Talking
to Children
About
Nuclear War

Talking to Children About Nuclear War

William Van Ornum

AND

Mary Wicker Van Ornum

CONTINUUM / NEW YORK

1984
The Continuum Publishing Company
370 Lexington Avenue, New York, N.Y. 10017

Library of Congress Cataloging in Publication Data
Van Ornum, William.
Talking to children about nuclear war.
Includes bibliographical references.
1. Atomic warfare—Psychological aspects.   2. Children
—Psychology.   I. Van Ornum, Mary Wicker.   II. Title.
U263.V36   1984   155.9′3   83-26299
ISBN 0-8264-0248-8
ISBN 0-8264-0247-X (pbk.)

See also pages ix and x, which constitute an extension of this copyright page.

Contents

Acknowledgments

The authors wish to thank those who contributed to this book: Betty Bumpers, Kayla Chase, Gerie Crocker, Donna DeMuth, James W. Douglass, Shelley Douglass, Thomas Douglass, Benina Gould, Rev. Theodore M. Hesburgh, Bishop Howard J. Hubbard, Penny Jaworski, Michael Leach, Dan O'Donnell, Nessa Rabin, Helen Rabin, Jules Rabin, Norman Reed, Jr., the Rev. Ken Sutherland, and Fred Tietze. And we thank the staff of the Vassar College Library, and the Rev. Russell M. Abata for his interest and encouragement.

We are especially grateful to William A. Wicker for his critical review of the final draft. His creative researching, insightful editing, and commitment to this project helped shape every page.

Grateful acknowledgment is also made for permission to quote from the following materials:

"An Anatomy of Hope" by Robert Mills, from *Journal of Religion and Health,* vol. 18, no. 1 (1979). By permission of Human Sciences Press, Inc.

"Faith, Hope, and Suicide" by Edward V. Stein, from *Journal of Religion and Health,* vol. 10, no. 3 (1971). By permission of Human Sciences Press, Inc.

"Growing Up Nuclear" by Albert Furtwangler, from *The Bulletin of the Atomic Scientists,* January 1981. Reprinted by permission of *The Bulletin of the Atomic Scientists,* a magazine for science and public affairs. Copyright © 1981 by the Educational Foundation for Nuclear Science, Chicago, Ill. 60637.

"The Impact on Children and Adolescents of Nuclear Developments" by William R. Beardslee, M.D., and John Mack, M.D., from *Psychological Aspects of Nuclear Developments*. Washington, D.C.: American Psychiatric Association, copyright 1982. Reprinted by permission.

(Letter) "Dear God, I love this funny world," from *The Clowns of God* by Morris West. Copyright © 1981 by Compania Financier Perlina, S.A. By permission of William Morrow & Company.

"Psychological Fallout" by Michael J. Carey, from *The Bulletin of the Atomic Scientists*, January 1982. Reprinted by permission of *The Bulletin of the Atomic Scientists*, a magazine of science and public affairs. Copyright © 1982 by the Educational Foundation for Nuclear Science, Chicago, Ill. 60637

"PT Conversation—James Fowler: Stages of Faith" by Linda Lawrence, from *Psychology Today*, November 1983. Reprinted by permission of American Psychological Association.

"What to Tell the Kids" by Thomas Powers, from *Commonweal*, 16 November 1981. Reprinted by permission of *Commonweal*.

"You Can Try to Make the World Safer for Your Children . . . Or You Can Turn the Page" by Judy Langford Carter, from *Redbook Magazine*, July 1982. Copyright © 1982 by the Hearst Corporation. All rights reserved.

Acknowledgment is also made to the following individuals for permission to quote from their works: Eric Chivan, Sibylle Escalona, Joanna Rogers Macy, Frances Peavey, Harris Peck, Charles Varon, Vivienne Verdon-Roe, and Steven Zeitlin.

Preface

Talking about nuclear war isn't easy—it's frightening, controversial, and deadly serious. The prospect of self-annihilation mocks our sensibilities and contradicts that most basic of all human urges, the will to survive; so much so, that many adults simply choose to ignore the issue altogether. Unfortunately, ignoring the grave possibility of nuclear war won't make the potential any less real: it's a fact of our lives.

Talking with children about nuclear war is even more difficult. Kids don't think the same way as grown-ups, and they can't unravel the complexities of the nuclear age with the practiced logic and cool rationality of some adults. (We say "some" because many adults feel just as confused and helpless as the children.) They don't understand the situation and ask questions. Some are afraid. The possibility of nuclear war is a fact of their lives, too, and they are continually reminded of it.

In *Talking to Children About Nuclear War,* we have carefully avoided positioning ourselves at any point along the political spectrum on this issue. Readers interested in analytical or ideological discussions about atomic warfare—or in suggestions for additional material to read, organizations to join, or specific actions to take to work for peace—are advised to look elsewhere for this information, which is prolific and of every conceivable viewpoint. We encourage involvement in seeking solutions to the nuclear problem, but some issues appear unresolvable and must remain matters of opinion. We focus on talking about the *feelings* this topic evokes, not on political postures.

Similarly, we do not debate the morality of nuclear arms; we offer instead a psychological examination of the human emotions and religious responses evoked by talk of nuclear war. Chapter 4, for example, offers a unique section called "Dilemmas and Dialogs," as a set of exercises for adults who think that nuclear issues are worth discussing with children.

Our approach to this subject involved many avenues. We have digested some of the important studies by primary researchers that have appeared in the scholarly journals, and we are grateful to these professionals for the opportunity to synthesize and present their work in a simple manner for the lay reader. In addition, we interviewed a number of adults who have shown great dedication in talking to children thoughtfully about nuclear war. Finally, the first author brings his background as a clinical psychologist working with children and adolescents, as well as adults, who face crises in their lives.

We believe that talking to children about nuclear war is a responsibility that should not be left to "others." We must care enough about our children to listen to them, pay attention to their concerns, answer their questions, and help them feel supported and loved by our willingness to face a difficult problem together with them with openness, honesty, and courage.

·1·

Wanting to "Do Something"

This book is for adults and young people who want to talk with each other about nuclear war, but don't know how.

Written by a clinical psychologist and a journalist who specializes in educational materials for young people, *Talking to Children About Nuclear War* takes as its starting point the feelings the threat of nuclear annihilation evokes in all of us. These feelings—fear, anger, cynicism, bewilderment, denial, despair—have a reality all their own which must be dealt with before we can take whatever steps to prevent war that are meaningful to us. This book hopes to inspire readers to begin to deal with their emotional reactions to thoughts or discussions of nuclear warfare, and to consider the feelings of those they love most. Topics for adults and young people to discuss are also suggested.

A nuclear bookshelf with more than 250 books about some aspect of the nuclear arms race has appeared within the past year.[1] Most offer a political perspective or present some sort of strategic analysis. Many tilt to the left; others lean to the right. Still others are careful not to align themselves with any partisan position and seek only to interest readers enough in the debate over nuclear armaments to get them to work toward finding a means of averting nuclear war.

Books on nuclear war generally point out the grim facts of the arms buildup (missile stockpiling, warhead counts, pros and cons of disarmament, etc.); describe the awesome and frightening effects of dropping the Bomb (degrees of destruction, radiation, fallout, etc.); argue the immorality of nuclear weaponry (it is contrary to the will of God); or advocate activism through a variety of means (political involvement, civil disobedience, passive resistance, public education, etc.).

In the complexity of these discussions, we sometimes forget that "the issue of nuclear war is an issue of the heart as well. No matter what your politics, you want the world to continue."[2]

Books about nuclear war stress that most of us have avoided the issue and need to be educated about it—because it is a fact of our lives. Readers are shown the urgency, the impending tragedy of the nuclear arms race. One dramatic way this is done (popularized by enterprising print and broadcast journalists) is to pick a familiar city, any city—your city—and graphically illustrate the effects of dropping an atomic bomb on it. Their goal is twofold: to prove that anyone who claims, "It can't happen here," is sadly mistaken, and to suggest that it probably will happen, so let's learn the facts and be prepared. As the introduction to one book tells us: "This section paints a picture of what nuclear war is all about. Chapter One, a fictionalized account of a nuclear attack on a city, makes unpleasant but necessary reading."[3]

Sometimes the unsettling truth about what is possible mobilizes us to work for peace. More often, though, it makes us bury our heads in the sand. With all the struggles and suffering each of us faces every day, who wants to contemplate instant incineration by a bomb falling from the sky? We deny the danger, blot it out, because life is tough enough as it is.

Another group of authors, most of them dedicated and sincere, approaches the nuclear threat from a theological or ethical viewpoint. Their goal is to foster a greater moral awareness in all of us, and they warn us of the insanity, the blatant immorality of what the human race appears to be doing to itself. These writers often appeal to religious traditions of nonviolence and pacifism, and strive to inspire us to build a better world. Unfortunately, by addressing only the moral or religious dimensions of nuclear war, some of them fail to examine the complex feelings of adults and young people alike, or offer advice on how to overcome a communication barrier that exists between both. Children tune out well-meaning adults who, sometimes stoic, sometimes preachy, spout facts, opinions, religious or political platitudes—anything but their gut feelings. Today's young people, for better or worse, are savvy and cynical. Old before their time, they know a dodge when they see one.

Psychology alone is not enough to help us cope with the specter of nuclear destruction; it is inadequate in helping us make moral decisions about war and peace, an exercise that the nuclear threat demands. Every person, in their own way, either works for peace, supports nuclear policies as necessary for national security, or remains indifferent or ambiguous on the issue. Each of these positions is a moral choice, not a psychological understanding.

Similarly, religion alone is an incomplete response. Peace, even temporarily, has never been achieved solely by religious inspiration. Religion may give us hope, put us in touch with something bigger than ourselves and thereby make us stronger. The problem occurs when religious people persistently focus on faith and hope without acknowledging our anguish about the prospect of thermonuclear war. Faith and hope are only meaningful when a *human* response to the nuclear issue is taken into account. People of faith must be given permission to be fearful, depressed, or hopeless. Not surprisingly, when clerics appear sanctimonious instead of compassionate, young people look elsewhere for answers.

Talking to Children About Nuclear War is unique in that it combines a psychologist's knowledge of human emotions and skills in communicating about stressful topics with the values of Christian teachings. It recognizes that adults who care enough to help children understand the threat of nuclear war from a religious context will themselves need help in doing so.

For people with a religious orientation, taking a stand on nuclear weapons is vital. Religious leaders and groups have played an increasingly important role in the growing movement to prevent war, and virtually every mainstream religious denomination in this country has backed some sort of peace resolution. In May 1983, the U.S. Catholic bishops issued a pastoral letter opposing nuclear armaments, calling for an immediate bilateral and verifiable nuclear weapons freeze, and recommending that peace education be initiated for Catholics of all ages.

Protestant and Jewish faiths have been equally outspoken. The United Presbyterian Church, the Episcopal Church, the United Methodist Church, the American Baptist Churches, the American Lutheran Church, and both the Union of American Hebrew Congregations and the Rabbinical Council of America have taken stands ranging from a ban on all nuclear weapons to mutual arms control and reduction.[4]

Religious persons cannot remain indifferent to nuclear war: they must deal with this issue on an intellectual level and translate their churches' mandates into meaningful political and social action; they also need to understand its emotional impact on their lives and the lives of those they love. From a psychological perspective, *Talking to Children About Nuclear War* examines the "psychic fallout" of living in the constant shadow of a terrible fate.

Why the focus on children?

Scientific research continues to mount: children are gravely affected by the fear of nuclear war. "A study by the American Psychiatric Association confirms that fear of a nuclear holocaust— either through war or a power plant disaster—is prevalent among children and adolescents. They speculate on whether they will have a chance to bring up a family. Their nightmares depict the end of the world."[5]

Sometimes a family finds it difficult to acknowledge debate about the country's nuclear policies because the family breadwinner is in the military, or works within the defense industry. Because such discussions invite questions about the source of the family's financial security, the issue is avoided. This can be seen as a "no-win" situation, especially when a parent is committed to or dependent upon a job that demands allegiance to a strong national defense. To consider, or even discuss, alternate ways to make the world "safer" could undermine the family's sense of financial stability. A difficult dilemma.

We know from psychology that children often adopt the attitudes of their elders. Recent surveys of American schoolchildren show that many believe there will be a nuclear war in their lifetime. The threat of nuclear war haunts all of us, but psychological studies suggest it is particularly distressing to children. Even children as young as five are often left to deal alone with their nervous curiosity. They are either reluctant to approach their parents and teachers, or ineffective when they do, because many adults are simply too uncomfortable with the topic. In a 1983 California study of 913 high school students, nuclear war ranked second only to a parent's death as a source of greatest worry. When asked who they talked with about their nuclear fears, "Seventy-three percent mentioned their friends, but few mentioned adults. Fifty-seven percent said they didn't talk about such things with parents, and the numbers were even higher when it came to teachers and counselors. A majority (56.4 percent) said their parents were also afraid of nuclear war."[6] Adults' unwillingness, or inability, to calm a child's fears contributes to this sense of helplessness and hopelessness.

Perhaps many children today experience the quandary of Anne Frank, who sensed a denial of the Nazi threat by most of the adults around her, yet could not follow their example: "For myself, I shall remain silent and aloof; and I shall not shrink from the truth any longer, because the longer it is put off, the more difficult it will be for them when they do hear about it."[7]

If children are distressed by the possibility of nuclear war and death at an early age, they are also alert to peace, and in a way adults may have forgotten. Children are absorbed in the simpler things of life that are peaceful and precious in their simplicity. They savor daily observations and occurrences that adults—preoccupied with responsibilities and worries at a different level and so jaded to life that their eyes are dimmed to its wonder—no longer seem to notice. At an international symposium on

"Children and War," held in 1983, a study was presented of Finnish schoolchildren who had been asked to draw pictures of peace. The children's conceptions of peace were often more subtle and complex than their pictures of war—there were no dominant images of guns, soldiers, or bombs. Instead, they drew people— ordinary people—doing various chores, walking in the street, or shopping. The figures looked happy. The schoolchildren startled adult interviewers with pure and uncomplicated definitions of peace:

- Peace. It means that the country is all right again and that the broken houses are whole, not in pieces as during the war and people are in peace and they needn't be at the front.

- I'd draw a white flag and put there people who are eating.

- A girl and her mummy.

- A house and summer and then I'd put there some grass and stones and then a small, you know, a white carpet which people can lie on.

- People who look kind; such people who laugh.

- A cat would walk and drink milk.[8]

In the United States, the "Children as Teachers of Peace Project," sponsored by Peace Links Worldwide, asked elementary schoolchildren to describe with words and pictures how they would help world leaders promote peace. One child responded:

If I were a teacher to the world's leaders, I would suggest that we have an endless piece of paper; call it the Treaty of Peace. Every citizen of every country would sign it. By signing this treaty, people would promise to work for peace for ever and ever.[9]

An eleven-year-old wrote:

If I was a leader, I would try to get all the leaders of the world to be friends. That way, if any of the countries got in an argument, they could talk and think about the situation to the rest of the leaders, or the countries could compromise. I would also try to get the leaders of the world to do away with

their war equipment. I would also try to get the factories that
make these war machines to make peace machines.[10]

The authors of this guide believe that our thoughts and feelings
about nuclear war must be acknowledged and dealt with in an
intelligent manner, but realize that in order to do this, many of
us must first understand our own reluctance to think or talk about
the issue, particularly with children. We need to be receptive to
the increasing evidence that children, in both their waking and
sleeping hours, think about nuclear war. We need to consider
why we treat the issue in a cursory or incomplete manner, or
ignore it altogether. Are we embarrassed because we're ill-informed? Are we uncomfortable expressing our deepest feelings?
Do we find the topic too depressing? Do we feel such talk will
"scare the children"? Are we so afraid of saying the wrong thing
to a child that we say nothing? Do we think questioning our
nation's nuclear policies is unpatriotic?

Whatever our reasons, we need to "get over the hump," as it
were; to work through our reluctance or denial before we can
take those vital first steps toward actually "doing something."
Then, if we choose to talk about nuclear issues with our children,
we will be able to talk on an emotional level as well as a factual
level.

The fear of nuclear war and suspicion that their lives may be
unnaturally shortened is as much a crisis for children as is the
trauma of death or divorce in the family, illness and hospitali-
zation, abuse, foster care, or family drug and alcohol problems.
Talking with children about the truths of their lives is indeed
difficult, often requiring all the strength and wit we can muster.
Yet avoiding, or glossing over, the facts does not help. One thing
is certain: *If we cannot communicate our understanding of their
experiences, our acknowledgment of their hurt, their fear, their
anger, our caring enough for them to admit the truth about their
lives,* then they will remain untouched by our efforts to reach
them. Mired in their crisis, they will fail to consider or adopt
necessary alternatives for coping.

Many adults, especially parents, face this challenge when talking with young people in crisis, and they will encounter special

difficulties when they try to ease a child's anxiety about nuclear war. A major coping mechanism of many adults is to deny the potential for their society's, their family's, and their own destruction. This has advantages. Denial helps us go on with our daily activities; it keeps us from becoming so frightened and overwhelmed that we find ourselves completely immobilized. In fact, therapists often encourage patients to concentrate only on that in their lives which can be changed. Brooding, depressed clients are counseled to redirect their attention from poverty and starvation in Asia, overpopulation in Africa, political oppression in Latin America, or man's inhumanity to man at home. Instead, they are encouraged to do "little positives" for themselves each day: take a walk at lunch, treat themselves to an ice cream or a new hairstyle, have coffee with a friend. Since many therapists view depression as a state of *learned helplessness*, being in control of the little things in life counteracts depression. Turning our minds and spirits away from things we cannot control can be healthy.

But the peril of nuclear war is different from all other problems in the modern world. It is the most pressing danger and the greatest moral dilemma humanity has ever faced. The Rev. Theodore Hesburgh, President of the University of Notre Dame and a leading Catholic theologian, is considered an authority on the subject. He has served on the National Science Board for twelve years, and was the Vatican's representative to the International Atomic Energy Commission for fifteen years. His opinions have been sought by politicians, pontiffs, and peoples of all faiths and convictions.

Hesburgh has this to say about what the threat of nuclear war means to the world: "This, unlike many problems, is a problem that affects every human on earth—man, woman, and child—and none of us can really stand back from it. Of all the problems we face, whether they be problems of justice, economic development, education, or equality of opportunity for minorities, one comes suddenly to the thought that if the nuclear problem is not solved, then all these other problems will disappear because there won't be any human beings left to have problems. That's a pretty sobering thought."[11]

It's a fact of our lives, and those of our children, that we could all expire instantly and unexpectedly in a nuclear war. Children *know* this, and need to talk about it. We asked one youngster if she felt there is any precedent in history for the way kids feel today. "Do you think this is a unique historical situation? Can it be compared to other trials people have faced in the past—wars, famines, plagues, persecutions—or is it a new ballgame for kids and adults?" Her reply: "It's a new ballgame in that it's the biggest ballgame ever."[12]

This child's understanding echoes Albert Einstein's warning of nearly four decades ago: "The unleashed power of the atom has changed everything save our ways of thinking, and we drift toward unprecedented catastrophe."

Thinking about the strange and unknown in terms that are familiar, and therefore reassuring, is a normal human response. In the face of the nuclear threat, however, it is woefully inadequate. Nations stockpile nuclear armaments as if they were artillery shells and bullets. They compare the size and strength of their nuclear arsenals with that of their rivals, operating under the Civil War military logic that victory is with whomever is "firstest with the mostest." Governments issue dubious civil defense plans which do not allow for heat, blast, radiation, and fallout effects of modern nuclear weaponry. They fail to recognize that the arms race is a race to nowhere, that in a nuclear war, there are no winners.

General Douglas MacArthur, having lived through the process of the military's technological leap from non-nuclear to nuclear weapons, said: "The very triumph of scientific annihilation has destroyed the possibility of war being a medium of practical settlement of international differences. No longer is war the weapon of adventure whereby a shortcut to international power and wealth can be gained. If you lose, you are annihilated. If you win, you stand only to lose. War contains the germs of double suicide."

Nuclear war is extremely difficult for the human mind to com-

prehend, and the question of arms control is inherently controversial. "On the one hand, it almost defies common sense for a
nation to compromise with adversaries over the composition of
its defenses. On the other hand, it comes naturally for Americans
and their political leaders to try and keep a rivalry that could
destroy the world from getting out of hand. Arms control appeals
to a peculiarly Yankee mixture of idealism and realism—a hard-
headed faith that despite ideological, political and military ten-
sions between the superpowers, they ought to be able to reach
contractual agreement on measures in their mutual interest."[13]

Medical and mental health professionals in this country have
expressed alarm at the growing potential for nuclear annihilation,
and the debilitating psychological effect this prospect has on our
population. Many have been using their professional expertise—
through education, counseling, and specialized knowledge and
training—to help citizens in every possible way to confront this
problem. They view this involvement as central to their social
responsibilities.

In addition, lawyers, teachers, scientists, students, clerics,
mothers, business and civic leaders, entertainers, journalists, art-
ists, social workers, environmentalists, politicians, public ser-
vants, and military leaders have banded together to lobby for a
solution to the nuclear problem. They have sponsored an unprecedented flood of teach-ins, workshops, demonstrations, ref-
erendums, discussion groups, legislative proposals, letter-writing
campaigns, petitions, films, and books addressing the issue.

The unleashed power of the atom is "the light of a thousand
suns." A new ballgame. A universal danger of unfathomable
magnitude, and a fear which touches each of us. It won't go away
if we avoid it. Our only hope is to confront it. By ignoring it, we
lose our chance to conquer it, and we lose the opportunity to
experience a unique sense of global community.

The strongest examples of community in human history have
occurred when people faced the prospect of death together. In
some ways, each of us is like Anne Frank, trapped in a darkened
attic, awaiting death. Although some of Anne's family and friends

denied the encroaching Nazi threat, Anne, her father, and many of the citizens of Holland did not. From their honesty and courage came a powerful spiritual experience. Their love for one another, their genuine sharing of feelings, and their bravery united them in community.

Anne's father was an enormous inspiration to her: he was cognizant of danger, truthful about its imminence, and took realistic steps to protect his family. His example gave Anne the strength to face a terrible fact of her life. She recorded early on in her diary: "When we walked across the little square together a few days ago, Daddy began to talk of us going into hiding. I asked him why on earth he was beginning to talk of that already. 'Yes, Anne,' he said, 'you know that we have been taking food, clothes, furniture to other people for more than a year now. We don't want our belongings to be seized by the Germans, but we certainly don't want to fall into their clutches ourselves. So we shall disappear of our own accord and not wait until they come and fetch us.' "[14]

The Franks transcended the threat. That threat brought them closer together; it made them stronger.

Parents everywhere face an urgent challenge to try to make the world safer for their children. Judy Langford Carter, a mother and contributing editor of *Redbook* Magazine, writes: "At times I feel the nuclear threat has nothing to do with me, especially when protecting the little bits of life for which I am directly responsible takes all the strength and wit I can muster. And I *can* protect them. I bundle them up to keep them out of the cold, hold their hands when they're frightened, feed them the kinds of food that will keep them healthy. I worry when they are out of my sight, worry that I should spend more time with them, plan more picnics, talk to their teachers more. And on and on it goes— the balancing, the juggling, the trying to do and be all the right things at the right time. I want to cover my ears so I can't hear the nuclear war talk. Life is hard enough without thinking about that too.

"But we would have to lock ourselves into bomb shelters to

ignore it. . . . Each new crisis, each new warhead, each new round of loose talk brings the 'unthinkable' closer. We are right to be afraid, but the fear of extinction must motivate us to rebel against death with all the capacity we have.

"And that's why I can't sit this one out. As one citizen my power may not be great, but I can join with others and together we become very strong indeed—strong enough to gain control over the nuclear threat, strong enough to save the world for ourselves and for our children and for each other's children."[15]

Talking to Children About Nuclear War suggests ways that adults can communicate openly and honestly with young people about the painful, ominous, and frightening feelings that nuclear war summons in all of us. Although excellent material is available to show us how to work for peace, either through disarmament or through a strong and effective nuclear deterrence, few tell us how to communicate the intensity of our emotions, or advance from there to some course of action.

The opening chapters of our book describe ways children think and feel about nuclear war, basing these observations and conclusions on questionnaire data and interviews conducted by researchers across the country. Because this topic touches chords of vulnerability in families as well as children, we also examine some family discussions on the subject. Chapter 4, "Talking Together," suggests practical points to consider when talking to children about nuclear issues, stresses the importance of keeping the child's age or developmental level in mind, and presents vignettes of children and adults engaged in discussion of nuclear war. Each dialog illustrates themes (avoidance, providing the facts, admitting feelings of helplessness) that are treated in detail throughout the book. In some of these conversations, genuine communication takes place; in others, it doesn't. A commentary follows each dialog. (This chapter in particular might serve as a syllabus for high school discussions, adult education meetings, family talks, or as a starting point for spouses who want to relate more openly with their children about the issue of nuclear war.)

Chapter 5, "From Despair to Hope," considers some of the

emotional responses the fear of nuclear war stirs in us, and looks at these concerns from a religious point of view. Our final chapter is a summary of this information, and it offers practical advice to parents and other adults who think that nuclear war is a subject worth discussing with young people.

Eric Chivian, a psychiatrist at MIT, has said, "Children are our conscience and our future. We must listen to them. We must not let them down."[16] We don't need to have all the answers. We don't need to be experts. Our task is to create a supportive environment in which children can express their concerns, understand our feelings, ask questions, learn the facts, and become stronger in the face of them. As family therapist Steven Zeitlin observes, the very act of talking with children about their fears of nuclear war is helpful, and in that alone, the family is "doing something."

·2·

It's a Fact: Kids Think About Nuclear War

Adults don't keep secrets from children very well. Sometimes kids know adults better than adults know themselves. Infants sense when their mothers are upset. Toddlers react to confusion and stress by becoming unsure and unhappy themselves. And the best way to get a teenager to broadcast family troubles is to pretend they don't exist. You can't hide the truth from children.

When adults don't let children voice their fears, these fears can multiply, or be acted out, indirectly. However, when adults listen to children's concerns, and when they help youngsters talk about their feelings in the context of caring relationships, children become less puzzled, less troubled. They feel cared about, understood, loved.

A child's sensitivity and alertness to hushed-up family problems or closet skeletons extends to rumblings in his or her larger environment. Children absorb bits of information about global problems from television, radio, newspapers, and magazines; from comments at school or play; from overheard conversations between adults. The word "nuclear" is part of their vocabulary, even if they can't quite define it. Mushroom clouds and a charred planet appear as graffiti in many cities. Youngsters piece together these fragments in a jumbled patchwork of mixed perceptions that make them anxious: "The world is not safe. If adults are scared and helpless, what chance do we kids have?"

Do we really succeed in sheltering children from our fears? Anyone who lived through the Cold War knows that, whether or not they ask questions, kids think about the Bomb in private. In the fifties and early sixties, children were coached to hold paper over their heads, hide under desks, look away from windows, or run to the nearest fallout shelter in the event of an atomic attack. Beyond that, they were not given information or explanations that made any sense to them. Adults didn't want to frighten them, but the lack of information and reluctance to talk had an opposite effect. One vivid memory of many young adults is Nikita Khrushchev's bellicose speech to the United Nations, when he pounded a shoe on the delegate's desk and threatened, "We will bury you!" Children saw him on television, in their homes, and watched their parents grow tense and angry. Although Khrushchev's reference was to economics, many Americans interpreted his words to mean that he was threatening war. It never occurred to adults that the kids were scared, too, and that their imaginations would wreak havoc with the little they saw or were told.

This limited introduction to the "Red Peril" was too cryptic. Children suddenly were apprehensive, didn't know what to expect, didn't know who or what the enemy was. In their minds, a dangerous bogeyman was loose. Would he suddenly appear in *their* town, come into *their* home, hurt *their* family? These questions were usually met with, "There's nothing for you to worry about." Our avoidance of meaningful discussion of the nuclear issue is much the same.

Michael Carey, a historian trained in psychoanalytical methods, interviewed adults who grew up in the forties and fifties to gauge the effects of nuclear weapons on their lives. "Fear of nuclear weapons," he reports, "could—and can—be embarrassing, rendering those who dread the bomb ludicrous if they express their emotions. A priest recalled hearing an air raid siren while walking home many years ago. He knew that if he ran to a shelter and there was no attack, he would make a fool of himself. He thought: 'I'm not going to be the first one to run. If I see somebody else running for cover, then I'll run.'

"A poet from Philadelphia still wonders if the loud sirens he hears as a normal part of urban life might be a warning that nuclear war is imminent. . . . 'You know,' he chuckled, 'these are what would be considered neurotic fears. Actually, the fear of nuclear war is a completely sane one, but I can admit this to you only because you admitted it to me.'

"A social worker from New York believed that the bomb was one of those powerful mysteries that embarrassed not only him but other people: 'And it probably embarrassed my parents, and they sort of communicated it to me—like sex, like death, like God, like certain things that happened in my parents' past that they did not want to talk about.' "1

Every society has its forbidden topics. In some, sexuality is a taboo. In others, religious doubt—or religious faith—must not be mentioned. Many families today have placed discussion, or even acknowledgment, of nuclear war off limits. It's too threatening, reminding parents of their own vulnerability. The family can end, instantly and without warning. "I come as a thief in the night"—the biblical admonition has assumed grotesque proportions, itching to be carried out by the hand of man instead of the will of God.

The absurd death victims of a nuclear blast would experience is perhaps the cruelest hoax of all. One educator asked a fourth-grade student if nuclear "issues" should be discussed in school. He did not mention the word "war."

"Yeah, for sure," the boy replied.

"Why?" asked the teacher.

The student turned and mumbled, "You really don't want to hear my answer." When assured that the teacher did, he said, "So that when we all get blown up, I'll know why it happened."2

Surveys and studies show that children are mindful of nuclear war. One doesn't need formal research, though, to identify violent themes—killings, bombings, and super-villains—in children's art-work, playground games, cartoons, comic books, and casual con-versations. References to nuclear warfare abound: "There's an atom bomb in my head!" or "There's a nuclear war going on inside me!"[3] To argue, as many adults do, that children are un-aware, untouched, and uninterested in society's "bomb culture" is to be blind to the facts and stimuli of our daily lives.

MAD magazine, in an issue satirizing nuclear war, goes as far as to suggest that youthful preoccupation with the Bomb is subtle and irreversible. Perhaps the best way for adults to see this is to envision a day in the life of a child. Adults attempting this must make a conscious effort to remain in touch with the alarming array of "nuclear stimuli" to which children are exposed. This isn't difficult.

Video games—those found in arcades and those played at home on personal computers—are tremendously popular with today's young people. Missile Command, Battlezone, and Defender are among the favorites, and their themes of technological warfare are taken for granted.

Television and cinema have always had a powerful impact upon youth, and the entertainment industry has not overlooked chil-dren's curiosity about nuclear war. The movie *WarGames,* in which a teen accidentally taps into a Defense Department com-puter and brings the world to the brink of nuclear disaster, was seen by millions of youngsters. It was such a box office success that it's now the basis for yet another video game, Thermonuclear War.[4]

And then there's music, probably the most potent of all external influences on the thoughts and behavior of young people. Popular rock music has been peppered with social and political criticism in recent years, and song lyrics deliver powerful antiwar/antinuke messages. In addition, many American communities now offer twenty-four-hour music video via cable television, and a signifi-cant number of these short films have antiwar themes. Rock su-perstars are among the most visible (and vocal) of all peace activists, and legions of their adoring fans have embraced the nuclear dis-armament crusade. The universal popularity of rock music alone offers solid evidence that young people are regularly reminded of the threat of nuclear war.

An irate father of two teenage sons complained when a popular rock musician devoted his entire appearance on a television talk show to a discussion of nuclear issues and a plea for audience participation in the antinuclear campaign. "That man is our kids' idol," the father bristled. "And there he was, telling young people across the country that he's terrified of a nuclear war, that we've gotta do something. Now what kind of message is that for a kid— when his hero admits he's frightened? He shouldn't be talking about nuclear war at all."

Adults who try to shelter their children from nuclear issues have already lost the battle. Robert Jay Lifton, Yale psychiatrist and author of *Death in Life: Survivors of Hiroshima,* explains: "When parents shield their young to protect them, it's usually an expression of their own adult 'numbing.' It's an attempt to push the subject away . . . And even if you succeed temporarily in protecting your school-age child, it's only a matter of time until some terrifying image, some deadly bit of information, leaps out from the television or newspaper headline."[5] Lifton believes it is better, albeit more difficult, to deal honestly with the nuclear issue as questions arise. "There has too long been a conspiracy of silence. And this conspiracy functions in families as well as in the public domain."[6]

The few studies conducted in the United States since the destruction of Hiroshima and Nagasaki verify that children's interest in nuclear war is nothing new.

In the early 1960s, during the Cuban missile crisis when air raid drills and bomb shelters were prevalent, researchers at Albert Einstein College of Medicine wanted to determine what children knew about the tense world situation. They interviewed children from first grade through high school. But according to psychology professor Sibylle Escalona, who reported the results of the study, "We did not ask the children any questions about war or weapons. We simply asked, 'In what ways do you think the world will be different ten years from now?'

"Around 70 percent of the children mentioned the Bomb, and

that they might not have a future. They answered, 'We might be dead,' or 'We might be living underground forever and life wouldn't be worthwhile.' The majority hoped that this would not happen, but almost all had incorporated the knowledge of what was then the most dreadful weapon one could imagine into their conscious thoughts about the future.

"There have been a number of different studies since then," Escalona says, "but what I find most astonishing is that, no matter who did it, no matter what the population, no matter what their particular approach, the percentage of children who say that they know about nuclear war, think about it, worry about it . . . has always been between 70 or 85 percent. Children of every age state very clearly their awareness of having to live on two levels, with the full, constant background awareness that none of their plans, none of their expectations may be realistic.

"What has *increased* over the years, as you compare studies," she continued, "is the number of children who report grave concern and anxiety about the prospect of nuclear war. When children are asked, 'Do you worry about nuclear war seldom, sometimes, often, or a great deal,' the proportion which answers 'often' or 'a great deal' has steadily risen."[7]

In the late 1970s, an American Psychiatric Association task force investigated the psychological reactions of children and teens living in a world where thermonuclear war is a constant danger. The study team distributed 1,000 questionnaires to elementary and high school students between 1978 and 1980, and conducted an additional 100 interviews for more detailed responses.

Harvard psychiatrists William Beardslee and John Mack authored the study. They found the students' comments to be "quite disturbing and demonstrate [that] the imminent threat of nuclear annihilation has penetrated deeply into their consciousness."[8] Some typical responses:

What does the word nuclear bring to mind?
"Danger, death, sadness, corruption, explosion, cancer, children, waste, bombs, pollution, terrible, terrible devaluing of human life."

"Nuclear means a source of energy which could provide the world with energy needed for future generations. It also means the destruction of marine life whose environment is ruined by nuclear waste. Also the destruction of human life when used in missiles."

Have nuclear advances influenced your plans for marriage, having children, or planning for the future?

"I don't choose to bring up children in a world of such horrors and dangers of deformation. The world might be gone two seconds from now, but I still plan for the future, because I'm going to live as long as I'm going to live."

"Nuclear advances are not always on my mind. My philosophy is that life is full of dangers and troubles and worries—I can't spend my time on earth a psychologically sick person, afraid that any moment I will die. I feel that I would refrain from having children, though, not because of thermonuclear threats—because I'm not crazy about children."

"No, not really, because if there is a nuclear war there is no sense in worrying about it because whatever happens will happen. The technology is there and it can destroy the world."

Have nuclear advances affected your way of thinking about the future, your view of the world, and time?

"I am constantly aware that at any second the world might blow up in my face. It makes living more interesting."

"I don't really worry about it, but it is terrifying to think that the world may not be here in half an hour."

"I am strongly against it because the people who are in control of it are not worth trusting the whole world in their hands! It's much too much power for one person to hold."

"I think that, unless we do something about nuclear weapons the world and the human race may not have much time left (corny, huh?)."

"Everything has to be looked at on two levels: The world with the threat of ending soon, and life with future, etc. The former has to be blocked out for everyday functioning because very few people can find justification for living otherwise. But [it] is always there—on a much larger scale than possibilities of individual death, car accidents, etc.—even though the result to me personally would be the same."

"It makes you wonder about how anyone could even dare to hurt others so badly."

"Quite definitely, I believe we should try to save ourselves; any form of suicide alters the future. It would end our race."

"I feel that everyone's views of the world and ideas of the future have changed somewhat. I feel that the future is very unsettled and a nuclear war could destroy the world in a short time."

"I think that a nuclear war, which could break out in a relatively short period of time in the far future, could nearly destroy the world."

"In a way it has. It has shown me how stupid some adults can be. If they know it could easily kill them I have no idea why they support it. Once in a while it makes me start to think that the end of my time in life may not be as far off as I would like it to be."

"Yes, I feel if men keep going on with experiments they are bound to make one mistake that could mean the end of a lot of surrounding cities and if severe enough the end of what we know today as the world."

Members of the study group wondered at times if the pessimism they encountered was prevalent among America's youngsters. Incidental reports appearing in various print media seemed to support their findings. Mack cites this teen's letter to an advice columnist:

> Dear Beth,
>   Why is this called the happiest time of our life? I have a lot of worries and so do my friends. I don't just worry about dates and studies, I worry about other things going on in the world. Suppose there is a nuclear war. Suppose the air gets polluted. Suppose there isn't any gas left when I grow up, if I get to grow up at all. I wonder why we go to school and work so hard if it's all for nothing. Some of my friends do drugs and drink because they say they aren't going to last anyway, so

why not? We're just kids and powerless to do anything about it. Did it always seem this way to teenagers?[9]

By no means are all young people in favor of nuclear disarmament or a weapons freeze. Like many adults, some youths believe that a strong and credible nuclear deterrence is the best way for the United States to prevent war. The Catholic Archdiocese of Chicago sponsored an essay contest for high school students in 1983 on "How the Issue of Nuclear Disarmament Touches My Life." While the vast majority of papers were sympathetic with the peace movement, a few were not. Here are some excerpts:[10]

I fear the horror of war as much as anyone. I know that a nuclear war would be more disastrous than any other war. However, there is hope if we give our support to a defense system which can prevent war by making the attacker's strategic problem a great gamble, and one that can save millions of lives in the unhappy event that a war does occur.

I feel, as a Christian, that it would be morally wrong to disarm ourselves. I believe that the way to peace is through military strength.

Considering the suspicion and fear that all countries feel toward each other, I think that the hope for nuclear disarmament will never become reality. Even if we trusted another country enough to believe it really had gotten rid of all its nuclear weapons (a very unwise decision in my opinion), there would be no possible way to prove or enforce this. Furthermore, even if one could be certain that no more nuclear weapons did exist, it would be very easy for a country to rebuild such weapons during a war. And if one country, sworn to disarmament, was losing a war badly, I seriously doubt that it would hesitate very long before employing its nuclear weapons. Therefore, I feel that the mutual distrust and fear between countries of radically different cultures will prevent them from making or keeping any promise to disarm: only the knowledge that other countries are just as ready to blow us up may deter the use of our nuclear weapons.

From my viewpoint, a nuclear freeze in our country, along with the buildup of Soviet arms, would put our country in a vulnerable position.

I agree with Pope Paul VI. I feel that, as Christians, we must take a stand against Soviet armed power and repeated aggression. As Pope Pius XII said in 1948, "A people threatened with an unjust aggression, or, already its victim, may not remain passively indifferent, if it would think and act as befits a Christian."

The communist government of the Soviet Union is not going to disarm its nuclear warheads if told to do so, for it would not strengthen the Soviet Union, and the Soviet Union does nothing that will not strengthen herself.

Nuclear arms are necessary. In order to maintain peace between two parties, each must fear one another.

Let's consider other research. MIT staff psychiatrist Eric Chivian and Boston educator Roberta Snow interviewed 150 youngsters from grades 1–9. They talked to them in groups, so they would not feel alone and would be comfortable speaking out. They interviewed them at school instead of in their homes or at the office, so they would see that their peers felt similarly, and would realize that adults were taking time to listen to them. Chivian, above all, wanted to hear the children's concerns, to draw out their feelings. In turn, he wanted them to realize that adults had not given up, and were taking steps to confront the problem.

The interviews were recorded on a videotape entitled, "There's a Nuclear War Going on Inside Me," a quote from a fifth-grader. Chivian filmed the interviews for several reasons. He wanted to show it to discussion groups, and felt it was important to document the children's nonverbal behavior (body language). He explained that throughout the taping, "We wanted to avoid the temptation to correct misinformation, to challenge the stereotypes kids have. And most of all, while this was being done, we attempted to *not reassure* them that everything was going to be okay. We wanted to record this experience as accurately and completely as possible. That was the hardest of all."[11]

Questions the psychiatrist asked included, "How did you first hear about nuclear war?" "Where did you hear about it?" "What does it make you think and feel?" "How does it affect your future plans?" Here are typical responses, beginning with a five-and-one-half-year-old first-grader:[12]

> Sometimes it really, like, scares me. Sometimes I hope there never will be one. I know there's been only two so far, World War I and World War II. And I hope there'll never be a World War III—whatever it is.

One third-grader recalls visiting an Army base with his uncle:

> He was gonna show me around. And then he was talking to me in the car when we were going home about how a few nuclear bombs could wipe out the whole world. It was real weird. It scared me. I was scared almost half the week because I thought a nuclear bomb was gonna fall down and blow up the whole world.

Another third-grader, with conviction in his voice, remarks:

> I think I'd rather live in B.C. where there were people, but no warkinds. I always keep on thinking that when I grow up I'm going to be an astronaut, but I think I'm never gonna be one. I think war's gonna keep on and that nuclear missiles . . . I think I'm gonna be dead and I'll never survive.

A seventh-grade boy:

> You know, it's so dangerous what we're playing with. And it really sounds like we're *playing* with it. I'm not sure what the issues are. I'm not sure whether anybody . . . knows if there *are* any issues [worth] arguing about that we have to use things like this.

A ninth-grade boy:

> I think it's gonna be someone from our generation that will change it. Because people . . . all of them must have their fixed opinions. We're growing up against it [nuclear weapons]. I don't hear any kids my age saying, "Yeah, yeah, let's go shoot off a few bombs." I mean, I don't really hear that many

old people saying that either, but they're the ones that have
them, not us. We don't want them. So if it's gonna be changed,
I think it's something for our generation, but it's gonna take
a little while.

Chivian and Snow studied the comments closely. They learned
that many first-graders worry about war, and saw all war as similar. Although apt to giggle during discussion, many admitted to
nightmares.

Third-graders felt helpless. They were interviewed during the
1982 Falklands War, and confused this conflict with a nuclear
war, which many thought was erupting. These youngsters fan-
tasized that they would be the sole survivors, and were keenly
aware that they might not grow up. There were fears of aban-
donment and loss of parents, family, and friends.

Fifth-graders displayed greater knowledge about nuclear war,
and also more anger: "Why don't we march?" "Why don't we
do more about it?" Early signs of despair were evident.

Seventh-graders reacted with cynicism and distrust of governments, civil defense plans, and the cool rationality of adults. They
wondered why we have weapons we don't plan to use, and in-
dicated a real willingness to involve themselves in peaceful solutions.

Ninth-graders felt angry, cynical, and helpless: "I don't want
to survive if everything else is gone." Or, "If someone makes a
mistake, we all have to die."

These children were acutely aware that they would pay the
biggest price in a nuclear war. They feared death at an early
age, and were terrified of having deformed babies. Milton
Schwebel, a psychology professor at Rutgers University who
studied the effects of nuclear war anxiety on youngsters, explains: "They would be denied a chance to live, to love, to work,
to bear children, and raise a family. They would lose, they felt,
the largest portion of their lives, and they would miss the
opportunity to enjoy the pleasures they had hardly even begun
to taste."[13]

Chivian is quick to point out that he doesn't feel nuclear anxiety is to blame for all youth problems today—rising child and teen suicides, drug and alcohol abuse, gang violence, etc. "But I think it's clear from our work, and the work done so eloquently in the sixties, that kids today are very much aware of the threat of nuclear war, and that affects them in such ways that we must begin to seriously ask ourselves whether nuclear weapons, just by their very existence, affect children in significant ways we cannot afford."[14]

Another researcher, Vivienne Verdon-Roe, is both a kindergarten and college-level educator. She spent six months interviewing children and adolescents for a book and documentary film entitled, "Growing Up in the Nuclear Shadow: What Can the Children Tell Us?" Verdon-Roe found that "many young people express a very real fear that their lives are going to be unnaturally shortened."[15]

Her study focused on children, ages six to eighteen, from diverse social and economic backgrounds. Each child told his or her fears about the nuclear arms race. Their statements were simple, direct, and from the heart. "The difference between adults' and young people's understanding of what nuclear war would really entail is apparent in how they speak of weapons," Verdon-Roe noted. "Adults tend to depersonalize them and refer to statistics, while a child thinks of a nuclear bomb as something that blows up people, imagining blood, mutilated bodies and dreadful suffering. We block off any consideration of such war because it is simply too painful to imagine."[16]

These children were angry at adults for jeopardizing their future. "How are we supposed to start our lives with death looking over our shoulder?" one seventeen-year-old demanded.[17] Others regarded national leaders with contempt and questioned the value of patriotism. "I think nationalism is a shame. Because of it, we're going to kill each other. I guess I can understand how the Russians feel—threatened. That's why they go bananas building up weapons, and that's why we go bananas building weapons. We all feel threatened."[18]

Yet Verdon-Roe discovered that, "In the interviews, it soon

became apparent that there was one basic difference between those children who felt hopeless and helpless, and those who were feeling positive and optimistic about their future. The former were not involved in any way in changing what causes them so much anxiety, while the latter were actively doing something to alter the situation."[19]

> I can't describe how it feels to be with other people who agree and are fighting for the same thing. It really is a sense of community, which gives me hope.[20]

> I think kids like myself, students who are not eighteen, have a lot of influence over what goes on. And I think there's a lot we can do, and we're not going to sit back and leave it to everyone else anymore. We're going to take some responsibility.[21]

These children emphasize that the way to lessen, and perhaps overcome, their feelings of despair and helplessness is through personal involvement. The counterpart of fear, they believe, is action.

Stepping back from the research that has been done, it is the impression of the authors that many of the studies were conducted with middle-class children. Perhaps future research could look more specifically at how children from less privileged backgrounds react to the nuclear threat. For the mental health professional as "scientist," further work could certainly be done to establish the relationships between children's thoughts about nuclear war and their socioeconomic level, their perspective-taking ability, the number of hours of television watched per day, the political and religious views of their parents, the intellectual development of the child, and so on.

In the course of our research, we interviewed fourteen-year-old Nessa Rabin, who lives with her parents and older sister, Hannah, in Plainfield, Vermont, a rural township of about 600. Nessa is a typical teenager (the day we talked with her she was upset about having to babysit and miss a band she wanted to hear). Although unusually articulate for her age, she is a normal schoolgirl who happened to believe strongly enough in something to take action.

In 1981—when Nessa was eleven—she, Hannah, and five friends founded the Children's Campaign for Nuclear Disarmament (CCND) while sitting at the Rabins' kitchen table. "We'd been talking a lot about the threat of nuclear war," Nessa remembers, "and how it was scary to us. We felt lots of kids around the country were as scared as we were, and instead of just worrying about it, we decided to do something.

"We wanted to involve as many kids as possible in an action that would allow them to express their fears of nuclear war and have their opinions heard. So at our first meeting we planned a children's letter-writing campaign. We asked kids all over the country to write letters to the President opposing the nuclear arms race. The letters were sent to the CCND office, and on October 17, 1981, a group of thirty children took the letters to Washington. All day outside the White House fence, we read each of the 2,832 letters aloud to people passing by."

The letters are powerful in their simplicity. Children this young are not encumbered by adult "logic." They speak from their hearts.

The youngsters tried to make an appointment with the President to deliver the letters. "The White House refused to acknowledge us," Nessa said, her voice rising. "That made us very angry. The White House wouldn't listen. It was scary, too, because, in a way, the White House is supposed to be our country's parents protecting us. And they weren't! They weren't listening to the scared children!" A meeting scheduled that day with the White House Liaison for Youth was cancelled at short notice. The letters were left with the mail room. Months later, a second meeting with the Liaison for Youth was arranged, in which CCND hand-delivered an additional 5,000 letters from children.

Nessa leaned forward and pulled her legs to her chest. "It was amazing," she said. "I would see the stacks of mail every day when I'd come home from school, after being with kids all day, and I'd read the letters—and kids were frightened. I always sort of knew that kids were afraid. You know, 'Mommy, what do I do if there's a nuclear war?' But nothing, *nothing* like what some of those kids were writing."

Although most of the letters were from children, a few adults wrote. Some sent messages of encouragement: "Great! Keep going!" Occasionally an adult would query: "Why are you doing this? Why are you scaring the children?" Or they argued: "You're wrong! We have to have weapons because the leaders of the Soviet Union are murderers." A few scolded: "It's all your parents' fault that you're doing things like this." Nessa's brow wrinkled. "That made us mad. Our parents didn't say, 'Why don't you start a campaign?' It was us kids. *We* wanted to do it."

Most of the 10,000 letters CCND has received came from children who wrote them as a school project, and more than half of these were from Catholic schools. "I think that's great," Nessa says, "because religion is a life-subject."

Adult reactions to CCND's efforts varied. "Our parents, and our adult friends in the peace movement, were very supportive. They'd say, 'Oh, great! Finally the kids, the kids too!' But others would say, 'Don't frighten my children,' or 'Children don't have to know about this.' And I understand," Nessa said. "If you're educated, as I want my kids to be if I have them, then you already know about nuclear weapons. And whether or not there's a nuclear war, you're living in this fear, and that's not a good thing to grow up with."

Nessa is upset by adults who say discussion of nuclear issues does not belong in the classroom. "That's irresponsible! I think it's natural that adults protect children, take care of us. If a history teacher or a social studies teacher will not talk about the nuclear issue, that's irresponsibility, and it's gonna hurt us in the long run."

Some adults, even those active in the peace movement, believe that very young children should not be engaged in discussions about nuclear war. But CCND's letter-writing campaign heard from children as young as seven.

"Little kids wrote," Nessa said. "They know about nuclear war, and they're scared. One of my close friends said to me, 'I don't think little seven-year-olds know enough to write; I think it's their parents behind them.' That may be. But seven-year-olds don't have to know the names of missiles, or how many weapons the Soviet Union or the U.S. has. That's what the government wants us to do, get caught up in technological jargon. That's dumb. To a seven-year-old, it's a matter of life and death. I think that's very innocent and very fine."

Does she believe there will be nuclear war in her lifetime? She draws a breath and pauses before answering. "Whew . . . um, I don't like to think about it, but it's very necessary to think about it. I think that whether or not it's planned, scientifically it's been proven that there will be, because machines are not perfect."

Nessa is frightened when adults ventilate their fears but don't offer hope. "One thing that scares me a lot," she admits, "is when people who are my idols politically—old activists, or my parents and their friends—when *they* get scared, that's very scary to me. I know that little kids cry when they're scared. But *adults?* It has to be bad."

After three years of work with CCND, including two letter-writing campaigns and participation in numerous peace marches and rallies, Nessa left the group. She was tired and wanted a break. "To come home every day after school and face letters from all these frightened children, and face adults who didn't know what to do about it . . . that's draining. I was becoming numb. Reading all those letters saying, 'Help! I'm scared. . . .' It got to the point where I'd just flip by them. Now I try not to think about it. This bothers me because I've become the person I was working against. I don't like to see inactive people. And I feel guilty. But I need some time off."

CCND's message is simple and to the point: Get rid of nuclear weapons. "Kids are afraid, there's no doubt about that," Nessa says. "It's a simple question, and yet it can't be, because if it was, something would have happened by now. I think that there has to be education. I don't think we have to memorize how many missiles or submarines each country has, or stuff like that. Education is a big word. I think if people were educated about *goodness, greatness,* they would not murder one another.

"Every tiny bit that people do makes a difference," she believes. "Maybe not to remove bombs, but to influence people of the world to remove bombs. I just wish that everyone could, at some time in their life—like next week—find the energy and the anger to do what us seven kids did. We influenced thousands of people, and if *everyone* did that, it wouldn't take too many people before the whole world knew."

Children like Nessa seem to understand a Soviet perspective better than adults. Says one pre-teen: "I feel sorry for the Russians. We both have nuclear bombs, but we're the only country in the world who has actually dropped one and killed all those people. We're scared of Russia, but they must be super-scared of us."[22]

Indeed, Artur Petrovski, a Soviet professor, offers evidence that Russian schoolchildren also worry about nuclear war. "Soviet children seem not to be different in this connection to the youngsters of other countries," he reports. "Certainly, everything depends on age. The small children do not know the causes of war and do not know how to assess the dangers that lead to the brink of war, but they feel the uneasiness of their parents and begin to look at the peaceful sky with caution. Who knows when a dangerous flame will flash from there?"[23]

Dr. Petrovski gives as an example a young Russian boy, eight or nine years old, who played a starring role in a Soviet film and was interviewed on Russian television. Asked if he planned to become a movie actor when he grew up, the youth thought a minute, then replied: "Well, yes . . . if I live that long . . . if there is no war."

Nuclear Weapons and Nuclear Energy

The relationship between nuclear weaponry and nuclear energy is frequently misunderstood by children and adults alike. This confusion is understandable: Both nuclear arms and nuclear power rely on the same technology. Both are extremely controversial and emotionally-charged topics. Both raise questions that are similar, yet different, from one another. Simply put, atomic bombs and atomic power are not the same, and it's important for adults to make that distinction when talking to children about nuclear war.

Many people who oppose nuclear weapons are also opposed to nuclear energy. They claim it isn't safe. Others are against nuclear arms but in favor of nuclear energy. They see it as the answer to America's (and the world's) energy problems. Still others support both. Given the disagreement and debate surrounding both issues—and the likelihood that "atoms for peace" and "atoms for war" will be eternally linked—it's vital for adults to be able to discuss intelligently with children the pros and cons of nuclear energy. Children must know the facts in order to clarify their feelings.

Adults who have read this chapter may be surprised to learn that so many children think about nuclear war. Young people reading this book will discover that they are not alone in their concerns. Some may feel differently than the youngsters whose voices we have presented.

Where do we go from here?

The following chapters suggest topics adults and young people may choose to consider if they decide to discuss nuclear issues together. We stress the importance of not trying to force children to talk, but to be available if they have things to say.

·3·

Family Vulnerability

Nuclear war is a family issue, one fourteen-year-old believes, "whether it's a family around the table or the family of the world. It's a lot of family issues—a grandma issue, a baby issue, a dog issue, a cat issue, a tree issue."

This girl's message is underscored every time the media reports on our nation's purported vulnerability to nuclear attack from outside aggressors. These reports evoke another kind of vulnerability, family vulnerability: the awareness of how precious, how fragile, how fleeting our time together as a family might be. When faced with this realization, many parents simply dismiss the issue: "There's nothing we can do about it, so let's not talk about it."

Children understand this reluctance. "I would find it hard to be a parent," one high-schooler admitted. "It's hard to tell a kid that they might die."

Benina Gould, a social worker with the Family Therapy Institute of California, has led workshops designed to help parents and children talk about their fear of nuclear war. She has found that most adults need to first come to terms with their own emotions—hopelessness, confusion, despair, doubts about their profession—before they can effectively communicate with children. One family she interviewed "had great difficulty talking about their emotions, even though they were very active in disarmament work."[1]

Despite parental avoidance of the subject, children's concerns about nuclear war can surface suddenly and unexpectedly in family situations. One father, irritated because his son wasn't paying attention to him, admonished, "You just wait until you're grown up and have children. You'll see what it's like. You'll see how hard it is." The boy replied, "I'm not going to have any because there's going to be a nuclear war and we're all gonna die." The boy's father was speechless. How much of that attitude is normal adolescent rebellion and how much is genuine belief in the ultimate destiny of his generation is hard to say. What is clear, however, is that the youngster was aware of nuclear war, and that the father was not prepared for such frankness from his son.

Putting worrisome topics out of mind can get us through the nitty-gritty of our lives. Fretting about Christmas bills in October won't lead us into a Merry Yuletide; balking at the expense of rearing children could mean we'd never start a family.

While denial and procrastination have a place, ignoring the unsettling subject of nuclear war can cause pain: it separates family members and helps build walls that prevent them from reaching out and supporting one another. Lack of communication, of shared feelings and strong emotions, can lead to isolation and indifference between family members and others with whom we come in contact. Stanford psychologist and author Philip Zimbardo is disturbed by this phenomenon: "I know of no more potent killer than isolation. There is no more destructive influence on physical and mental health than the isolation of you from me and us from them. It has been shown to be a central agent in the etiology of depression, paranoia, schizophrenia, rape, suicide, mass murder. . . ."[2]

Or as one child, who burst into tears at the thought of nuclear war and was comforted by family and friends, put it: "I think that's real important, because to be alone and freaked out is not too good."

What would have happened if Otto Frank, whom we mentioned in Chapter 1, had pretended that there were no Nazis, that there wasn't a war, and denied to his family the likelihood of their fate? Suppose one of the family rules—as Mrs. Frank would have liked—

was not to talk about depressing things? Each of them would have been locked in a separate, lonely cell of heart and mind, distant from each other, knowing deep down that the threat was real, yet unable to reach out for the love and understanding that would make them stronger.

Steven Zeitlin, a psychologist and family therapist, interviewed families in their homes about nuclear war. He approached them modestly, not as an expert with answers but as a fellow human being with similar worries. Before beginning the project, Zeitlin wondered how receptive these families would be. Many controversial topics cause divisive family rifts. We all know what happens when an unpopular topic is broached at the dinner table.

Would the families mind this seeming intrusion on their privacy? To the contrary, they seemed almost relieved that he had come to visit, welcoming someone who would "just start to mention the unmentionable." Common bonds were reaffirmed as family members realized, like George and Emily Gibbs in *Our Town,* that it's the simpler things in life we cherish most, and that we usually take for granted until they've disappeared.

"Tremendous courage, resourcefulness, and creative problem solving can be generated when a family faces its vulnerability together," Zeitlin believes. "I think the cost of denial within the family context is to greatly intensify feelings of powerlessness and despair. And as parents, one of the most painful things to face, I believe, is the limits on our ability to protect our children. I believe all parents face such limits, and I'm sure they faced them in all historical ages.

"In the last several years," Zeitlin continued, "my wife and I have encountered these limits in a particularly painful way. In 1980, we discovered that our five-month-old son, who at the time appeared quite normal, had a fatal genetic illness. The first two thoughts that crossed my mind when I learned that were, 'Would I have the strength to survive what I had to go through?' and 'What an outrage it was that such an event would intrude into the life of my daughter,' who at the time was three. I felt sick that I would not be able to protect her from the horror of what we'd have to go through, and I was terrified that it would ruin her life.

"In an analogous way, I think, the threat of nuclear war makes us all vulnerable as parents. It's a horrible reality and a horrible idea that intrudes into our lives and the lives of our children. We're all hostages, and as much as it hurts to face that vulnerability, if we don't, we run the risk of giving our children the message that we don't care about them."[3]

Some of the parents Zeitlin interviewed were at first anxious because they weren't well-informed about nuclear arms or foreign policy. They feared they'd be awkward or ineffective in a discussion, but were pleased to discover that their lack of knowledge was not a handicap in communicating with their family. They did not have to be experts; they did not have to have all the answers. Their children responded positively to their overtures. The very act of talking about nuclear issues showed that these parents were not helpless, that they had the courage to confront the problem, that they felt it was something worth discussing.

Interestingly, sometimes children were embarrassed to bring up their concerns, and surprised at what happened when they did. In one family, a nineteen-year-old son had never revealed, prior to the interview, his wish to attend the June 12th (1982) march in New York to protest nuclear war. His parents were strict, and he assumed that they would disapprove of this "radical" act. When he told them, his mother responded, "But I marched in the Civil Rights movement," and encouraged his involvement in social concerns. His father added, "I'm glad he's just not thinking only about how cold the beer is."[4]

In another family Zeitlin visited, two teenage brothers were teasing each other throughout the interview until asked what each thought the chances of a nuclear war were. "Fifty-fifty," they answered after pausing thoughtfully. All siblings fight, tease, and argue, but these two ceased for the last half hour of the interview after acknowledging the seriousness of their concerns.

One father considered building a bomb shelter. Deep down, he felt this wouldn't make much difference, but symbolically, it stood for the love they had for each other, a place to die together.

Many adolescents see little value in striving for personal gain and improvement; they expect a nuclear war to interrupt their life and end it prematurely. "Sometimes I feel real depressed, like there's no point in going to school, because I'm going to die soon. A lot of times, I'm really convinced that I'm going to die in a nuclear war." Or, "Once I found out what was going on . . . it seemed to me that everything was useless. There was nothing worth doing except living for the exact moment."[5]

Others are hell-bent on coping. One teenager designed a space ark to rescue survivors of a nuclear holocaust. Another reported that his friend is learning "survival training" so that he can live in the wilderness while city dwellers perish in a nuclear attack.[6]

Perhaps the biggest fear among children is that of losing their parents. One eight-year-old girl saw the movie *WarGames* with a group of her friends. When she returned home, she told her parents that she had enjoyed the movie, that it was exciting. That evening, shortly after the family retired, the girl wandered into her parents' bedroom. Her father walked her back to her room and offered to leave the light on when he left. The girl resisted— she didn't want her father to leave.

"Was there something about the movie that upset you?" her father asked. "Are you scared?"

"No, Daddy," she answered, "it wasn't a scary movie. But please don't leave me alone. I just want to be with you."

The movie had awakened fears the child didn't understand. All she knew was that something was terribly wrong in the world, and she needed the reassuring presence of her father before she could sleep.

Conversely, and not surprisingly, the greatest fear of parents is that of losing their children. Albert Furtwangler, a humanities professor at Mount Allison University in Canada, has written about his experience of growing up in the nuclear age, and how his world changed when his first child was born.

Furtwangler was raised in Seattle during the fifties, a time when civil defense and air raid drills were commonplace in schools.

(Seattle is the home of several major defense contractors and military installations; therefore, it's viewed as particularly vulnerable to enemy attack.) "We learned local geography thinking through its obliteration . . . Church and Sunday School might preach hell-fire and the end of the world; the public schools made [this] palpable."[7]

Fortunately, Furtwangler had a teacher who acknowledged his students' fears and also provided inspiration. "We could either wallow in the fear of dying at the end of the world, or we could get on with our work and hope to be in touch, as he was, with another generation."[8] Furtwangler carried on with his life, and when his first child was born, he reflected on that event in the vernacular of a generation raised in a nuclear society: "Other matters faded in that new light. Clean diapers piled up instead of books on the desks where we were writing. Meetings, concerts, and studies yielded to feeding times. Friends and family rearranged themselves. We encountered each other differently and more deeply. Every hour of our days was dislocated, interrupted—what is the word I want: irradiated?—by the growth and grasping hunger of a child we had begun but hardly knew.

"The controlled release of nuclear energy—what a joke! The thought occurred to me one spring day in my last term on campus. I was walking home, and I let my mind play over the obvious balances and antitheses. The half-life of uranium is one thing, however long that might be; but the whole life of a child is another, giving way to a grandchild, and so on and so on. A few particles of matter hold the potential for destroying the earth; a few particles of human life are the seeds for its fulfillment. The vast arsenals of bombs and missiles are growing obsolete in their secret silos; the children here on this playground are growing taller in the sun."[9]

The finality of nuclear war is an excruciating topic for families to acknowledge. Basic family security—the ability to protect their children and care for their elders—is called into question. The specter of nuclear war raises doubts whether the family will continue into future generations. Indeed, "every relationship along the great chain of being is in some degree affected."[10] One teenager voiced his objection to the way adults have placed his future in jeopardy. He said:

> I went to a conference on nuclear power a while back. At least fifty people stood and talked about the horrors of a nuclear war. However, through all the talk of the scientists, and experts, and religious leaders, and political leaders, I kept thinking, "What about us? What about the generations that really have to live with this fear?" About four hours after this had begun, an eleventh-grader from Plymouth, Massachusetts, got up and with a shaking voice explained to about 300 adults what it felt like to have your whole life set-up based on the fear that the world just might not be around for you to grow up in. He said, "No one should have the right to choose whether an entire generation gets to grow up or not." What can possibly be more simple. No one has the right.[11]

In addition to their concern for the human race, many children expressed grief at the thought of the destruction of the planet itself, as the following letter indicates.

> Dear Mr. President,
> I know you're probably proud of man's knowledge, but man's knowledge is destroying the Earth and the Earth doesn't just belong to man. If we get into a war, I'm just not worried about me and my family or people. If we want to destroy ourselves, we should do it without nature.
> When I think about the way people treat the Earth and the way animals treat the Earth, I find a big difference.[12]

Some mental health professionals hypothesize that nuclear weapons, simply by their existence, contribute to recent increases in family instability. They theorize that it may be a factor in the growing number of marriage breakups, the trend toward experimental marriages and alternate living arrangements, and the decision of many couples not to raise families. Family values of past generations no longer seem to apply. Robert Jay Lifton, Yale psychiatrist, has commented, "Once more the weapons tarnish and taint; spiritually they destroy and kill, even without being used."[13]

In a study regarding the emotional and social effects of the nuclear threat upon children, Vivienne Verdon-Roe reported: "Some young people criticized their parents for not having mentioned war/peace issues; they questioned how much their parents cared for them if they were not carefully evaluating their future. They apparently had not recognized that their parents might not be able to acknowledge the lemming-like (self-destructive) characteristic of the arms race because they are too paralyzed to do so, or that they might not discuss issues with their children in order not to alarm them. But several teenagers did address the question of frightening children."[14]

Children interviewed "contended that discussing nuclear issues was a good release for them. They want support as they come to grips with the nuclear-armed world they are inheriting. So it is very important for parents to be honest. Kids do not want to be told there is nothing to worry about if they suspect that there is. That sort of response," Verdon-Roe says, "will merely result in the child's distrust of your answers to other questions. Kids already know [about the nuclear threat]. I think it's more terrifying not to talk about it. Mystery is the worst thing possible. Being left alone to deal with it—that's much more frightening."[15]

Jules and Helen Rabin, parents of Nessa, the CCND founder mentioned in the previous chapter, have some thoughts on how parents can talk to their children about difficult subjects.

"I think it's difficult to start from scratch on any issue like this," Mrs. Rabin begins. "If you sit down with your kids and say, 'Well, now, here's the lowdown on politics, or sex, or anything . . .' it's very difficult to do it like that. But when issues are commonly dealt with on an everyday basis in the family, then it's a whole lot easier.

"I can't recall when our kids first became aware of nuclear war. I *can* recall not wanting to talk to them about it, because I really couldn't bear to think about it at all. And I certainly didn't know what to say to them. But we had talked about causes in general quite a bit, and we'd talk about war. Our kids grew up when we were very much involved in thinking about the war in Vietnam and taking some action.

"So they were certainly used to difficult issues being talked about. Hannah and Nessa didn't have a protected childhood. But I wouldn't know what to say to parents who *don't* talk about scary issues with their kids. I just think it's a bad idea to try to protect children too much. I mean, kids are awfully smart, and they know when you're hiding stuff.''

Jules agrees. "I think that if you didn't begin five years ago, then you'd better begin today, and avoid what Helen says you should avoid, and that's sitting down and saying, 'Son, I have some very serious things to talk about.' And then you bring him into the library, and you close the door, and then you sit down and have a serious man-to-man talk. It needs to have started naturally.''

He compares a parent's initial discussion of nuclear war with children to that of sex education. "I think that most kids have a kind of background awareness or anxiety regarding the nuclear issue—it's in the air, and rightly so. And I think, as with sex, it's appropriate to talk about these things as they come up." But he's quick to add, "Another bad way to begin a discussion is to take a three-year-old who hasn't even begun to think about sex and sit down with him and hammer away at all the different implications of that. You should answer questions as they arise for the child, but you need to have established a pattern of openness and communication between yourself and the kids so that they raise questions about things in the back of their mind—like sexuality or nuclear war.''

The Rabins feel it is important for parents not to exclude children from their conversations with other adults. When their daughters were young, the Rabins took them wherever they went—to parties, meetings, traveling. Rarely did they hire a babysitter.

Jules taps the table at which he and Helen are seated. "This kitchen table has been important to us," he reflects. "When we invite guests—grown-ups—the kids sit around, and they hear about things. And I think that's very old-fashioned and very good.''

Perhaps family discussions of nuclear war will always be difficult. It is a normal reaction to a frightening thought. But as Dr. Helen Caldicott, mother of three and president of Physicians for

Social Responsibility, advises: "To know is terrifying, but not to know may be fatal."

George Fitchett, a hospital chaplain who spends his daily rounds with patients who are dying, encourages others who want to enter that field of work but feel "uncomfortable" about it. "My own advice is more paradoxical. I do not think we have to become more comfortable with our own mortality. In fact, I am convinced that it is impossible . . . I believe that those of us who attempt to be with and care for the dying will be able to do so only when we have had a change of heart, when we have experienced the impossibility of doing what we hope to do."[16]

This outlook may give us courage in starting to discuss the gravest social and moral issue of our time.

·4·

Talking Together

Betty Bumpers, wife of Arkansas Senator Dale Bumpers, was a teacher in the late fifties and early sixties when civil defense "duck and cover" drills were commonplace. "I was very aware of the destructiveness of the nuclear age," she recalls, "even though I thought of the atom bomb as vaguely friendly because it brought my sweetheart home from the South Pacific. Those drills made no sense to me. I knew from reading that everyone would die when they saw the flash anyway."

Because she was reluctant to "scare the children" with this knowledge, Bumpers simply told her students they were practicing tornado drills, as the procedures are similar. "This evasion of the truth didn't ring quite true in my head," she remembers, "but I didn't do anything about it. It was one of those things where I was aware of the problem, but wasn't relating to it.

"I went along like this blindly for many years, until one day my nineteen-year-old daughter, Brooke, asked a question. In addition to her concern over the Trident missile accident in our home state, and then the Three Mile Island [nuclear power plant] incident, she had been deeply affected by a movie about the Nazi holocaust and how victims had lost track of their families. So, during a long drive back from Washington, D.C., to Arkansas in 1981, she asked without warning, 'Mother, we're such a scattered family. I wish while we're home this summer we'd sit down and figure out what we'd do in case of a nuclear disaster. Where would we find each other?' "

Bumpers rolled her eyes. "I almost ran up a tree, that question startled me so. I drove a while in silence and thought, 'My God, how do I handle this?' Then I said as casually and light-heartedly as I could, 'Well, honey, I guess we'd all meet back home in Arkansas.'

"Well, that *really* set her off. She said, 'My God, Mother, don't be so stupid! *What if Arkansas isn't there?*' "

From that point forward, Bumpers's life changed. "That question hit me hard, made me realize how we adults sweep our fears about possible extinction under the carpet while our children, who haven't yet developed these skills in concealing or rationalizing, *live* with it."

Bumpers realized that her daughter knew more about nuclear weapons than she did. "Brooke quickly informed me that Arkansas doesn't stand a chance, with seventeen Titan missile silos, two SAC bases, and a manufacturing and storage facility for toxicological weapons. She said these were all triple-targeted. Well, I didn't know what triple-targeting was, and I didn't know the difference between a kiloton and a megaton. I had just never bothered. I assumed someone else was taking care of national security—my longterm future and her longterm future. I just assumed someone would always take care of me, until I was struck by the realization of what a nuclear confrontation would mean."

This mother-daughter conversation stirred Bumpers to learn more about the arms issue. She began reading, attending workshops, and asking "some really tough questions" of her husband and other public officials. She eventually founded Peace Links, an international organization which encourages women's groups to add nuclear issues to their agendas. Her primary goal is to make parents and adults more willing and better able to talk with children about nuclear war.

"I know how painful it is," she says. "I'm scared, too, but I have hope. I believe we can turn this thing around, but we've got to talk about it first. We've got to face our own fears, that's the only way we can begin to understand them. If our kids bring the topic up, it's vital that we talk to them about it. Our kids know more than we think they do. They need to be able to articulate their fears. If we start doing something to change things, then we can communicate hope to them.

"Moms and dads are the most trusted people in a child's world," Bumpers says. "When kids see that adults care enough to talk things out—even if it's a little bit at a time—and try to do something about the situation, then that makes the child's world a safer place."

Many women tell Bumpers that they are ill-informed and overwhelmed by the nuclear issue, and therefore not competent to discuss it. " 'All right,' I say, 'Look into it a little bit and study it a little. This is not an issue where you need to be a technical expert. You don't need to be an expert in anything but loving your children.' "[1]

Caring adults want to calm the fears of their children, but sometimes have difficulty doing so because the topic is so painful. Yet research shows that denial of unpleasant truths greatly increases children's sense of anxiety and isolation.

Frances Peavey and Charles Varon, in "How to Talk with Your Children about Nuclear War," relate an incident about a father who went camping with his wife and young daughter.[2] As the family was sitting under fragrant white pines, the girl asked, "Will we be safe from the Bomb here, Daddy?" The father, taken aback, only mumbled. His daughter then climbed into her mother's lap and began sucking her thumb—a habit she had long since relinquished.

Peavey and Varon ask, "What if, instead, the father had taken his daughter in his arms, sat down, and said: 'No, we won't be safe here. There's no real protection if a bomb falls here. I don't think a bomb will fall today, but it frightens me as much as it does you. But no matter what happens, we're here together and we're going to take care of each other. Do you want to talk more about this?' "[3]

One can compare the attitudes of children surveyed about nuclear war to those of terminally ill children queried about their illnesses. In both cases, adults often try to protect the children—and themselves—from very painful feelings. A "conspiracy of silence" surrounds the youths. Adults who know that a child is near death may make a valiant effort to shield the child from his or her prognosis, but their false cheerfulness or evasiveness, however well intentioned, usually betrays their anguish. Children almost always sense this, and may think that an open expression of fear will meet disapproval. They play the game by adult rules.

What can we learn from children with terminal illnesses? Research shows that they not only are more anxious than other hospitalized children, but also dwell more on their condition. When asked to tell a story, they sometimes tell one with themes of loneliness, separation, and death—even though they never had directly expressed these fears to hospital personnel. This story was written by a child who knew he was dying, but hadn't been told the seriousness of his condition:

> This is about a woman. She's somebody's mother. She's crying because her son was in the hospital, and he died. He had leukemia. He finally had a heart attack. It just happened—he died. Then they took him away to a cemetery to bury him, and his soul went to heaven.
> The woman is crying. But she forgets about it when she goes to bed. Because she relaxes, her brain relaxes. She's very sad. But she sees her little boy again when she goes up to heaven. She's looking forward to that. She won't find anyone else in heaven—just her little boy that she knows.[4]

Saddest of all is the dying child's belief that nobody cares, a feeling stemming from parents' and doctors' feigned cheerfulness and lack of honest communication. Children will mistake this for a lack of love and concern, and therefore feel utterly abandoned. Ron Klingbeil, a thirteen-year-old dying of leukemia, wrote this letter to doctors and nurses. The Cadillac, Michigan, *Evening News* published it shortly before his death.

> I am dying . . .
> . . . No one likes to talk about such things. In fact, no one likes to talk about much at all . . .

I am the one who is dying. I know you feel insecure, don't
know what to say, don't know what to do. But please believe
me, if you care, you can't go wrong.
Just admit that you care. This is what we search for.
We may ask for whys and wherefores, but we really don't
want answers.
Don't run away. Wait. All I want to know is that there will
be someone to hold my hand when I need it.
I'm afraid . . .
I've never died before . . .[5]

However, nuclear anxiety is not the same. The possibility of
death is just as real—children know this—but it's not a certainty.
So why mention it? Odds are we will all live out our lives without
experiencing nuclear destruction. Helping parents and children
interpret their fears of death should not replace encouraging the
family to plan for years of happiness. Adults must marshal positive
forces and instill in their children a positive attitude.

When we consider nuclear war, we confront a crisis which requires a truthful stance and, as Erich Fromm puts it, "a revolution
of hope." This means acknowledging the threat and our qualms
about it ("Yes, there's a chance I'll die"), but focusing on the
positive ("But there's also a chance I'll live"). It means working
steadily with the things within our control instead of succumbing
to those beyond it.

Giving Children Support

For adults to realize that children know when they are seriously
ill or worry about the threat of nuclear war is one thing; to be
able to talk competently and sensitively with them about it is
another. Both topics require that we know how to help them face
crises: events that originate outside themselves, but which intrude
upon their lives and undermine their emotional and physical well-
being.

Dr. Elisabeth Kübler-Ross, a psychiatrist who has led the way
to a deeper understanding of the needs of dying people, says one
of the greatest challenges facing those in her profession is devel-
oping the ability to "hear our patients." Because of our tendency

to console or protect the dying with an "all is well" attitude, "our approach often neglects their very painful emotional and spiritual turmoil."[6]

Many adults confuse being supportive with offering simple words of encouragement ("Hang in there, kiddo, it's gonna be alright") or words of sympathy ("Gee, it must be tough"). Unfortunately, these expressions of encouragement or sympathy are often conditioned responses dictated by social custom. They do not communicate to the child an understanding of his or her experience, or reflect that understanding back to them. Nor do they imply that the child has the resources with which to face the problem.

When people are hurting, confused, troubled, anxious, alienated, terrified, doubt their self-worth or are uncertain of their identity or future, genuinely supportive comments will help them feel understood, which in turn will activate strong and positive responses.

Why We Don't Want to Talk About It

Thomas Powers, a columnist for *Commonweal,* doesn't talk to his three young daughters about nuclear war. What makes this particularly noteworthy is that for years Powers wrote essays on the arms race, and has authored a book on strategic weapons.

"Adults are practiced in denial, but children are defenseless," he says. "Once something is vivid in their minds, it's right there in the room."[7] He tells how he frightened his youngest daughter with an overly dramatic reading of *Little Red Riding Hood,* in which he lingered too long on a description of the wolf's sharp teeth and powerful jaws. He relates an incident in which a cruel man threatened his father (two years old at the time) by flashing a pocketknife in his face and hissing, "I'm going to cut your ears off!" This haunting memory has remained with his father for more than eighty-seven years, and the old man retells it as if it happened this morning.

Traumatic childhood experiences like this worry Powers. "I don't want to tell my children what nuclear war would do to them. I don't want them dreaming about it. I don't want them burdened with terrifying images that never fade. They need to grow up first, and get some practice in ignoring things they can't do anything about. They need to learn to hear without hearing, as adults do."[8]

Powers is uneasy when visitors to his home bring up the subject of nuclear weapons, or his book. "I try to change the subject, or skate over the details. I grow irritable. Don't they notice *kids* are around? Don't they realize there are some things you just don't tell kids?"

Yet Powers acknowledges that "kids get the point anyway. They pick things up. They don't really need to be told . . . All the same, I try not to talk about it. I don't want to be pressed about this."[9]

There are many objections to adults and children becoming involved in discussion, education, or activities relating to nuclear weapons and war. Milton Schwebel, the Rutgers psychology professor, commented on some frequently cited reasons:[10]

—*It hasn't happened yet, so it's better not to dwell on it.* As some adults are fond of saying, "Let sleeping dogs lie." Perhaps they are unaware of the efforts of those who have frantically worked to control near nuclear crises in the past.

—*Acknowledging nuclear fears will kindle anxiety in children.* One student pointedly responded to this contention: "We *should* be anxious. We've been lucky so far. How long can that go on? I put it out of my mind. I guess we all do. We shouldn't."

—*Children are too young to comprehend what nuclear war entails, let alone the enormity of the threat it poses to their own, and their family's, security.* If this were true, it might constitute a reason for not educating children about nuclear issues, but when we know that even elementary school children report nightmares about the end of the world, it seems realistic that adults be upfront about the topic.

—*It is unpatriotic to participate in discussion or reading which question our country's foreign policies.* "In fact, the contrary is correct. If our children are to develop as responsible people and intelligent citizens, they need to be able to be critical."

"My Concerns, or the Kids' Concerns?"

Some adults think that children who express concerns about the possibility of a nuclear war are being used as political pawns and do not have any real understanding of the issues. When told that surveys show that children think about nuclear issues whether we like it or not, one adult charged: "I know why those kids are afraid of nuclear war. It's because their parents and teachers grew up in the sixties, and they're still hung up about war. I'll bet lots of kids are just picking up the worries of adults around them." In another instance, at a symposium entitled "Today's Child: Growing Up in a Nuclear Age," a grown-up asked a child if youngsters like him might be parroting the concerns of their parents. The youth was quick to answer: "Totally untrue. We want it [peace] as much as you do because we're going to have to grow up and live with it."[11]

Such skepticism is not uncommon, and it does raise an important question for many parents and teachers: "Am I projecting my worries onto the kids, or do they have legitimate fears of their own?" Perhaps Kübler-Ross's counsel to those who work with the terminally ill best addresses this uncertainty: "It is essential that everyone caring for the dying and their families understand at all times their own concerns and anxieties in order to prevent a projection of their own fears."[12]

John Darr, a fifth-grade schoolteacher who has written on the subject, believes that "how a child experiences the nuclear threat depends upon the adult environment through which this threat is filtered to him." He suggests some possible adult responses to this threat, and their possible effect on children:[13]

—*Adult anxiety, but no child anxiety.* In this situation, the adult may "stir things up."

—*Adult anxiety, child anxiety, but the issue is not talked about.* Parents who are able to block out their fears and concentrate on everyday activities may create for themselves a comfortable aura. Consequently, "a child in this environment is not apt to feel anxious about nuclear war, but when he leaves this environment for one in which the nuclear threat is made more evident to him, he may develop anxiety with which he is ill-prepared to cope."

—*Adult anxiety, with disclosure of fear and helplessness, and child anxiety, with similar expressions of fear and helplessness.* In this situation—and we believe that it occurs frequently—both parents and children admit their anxiety. However, it's the child who experiences the more intense fears.

—*Adult anxiety, tempered with a willingness to try to prevent war.* In this situation, parents and children share anxiety, but find relief in the faith that something will be done to meet the nuclear challenge in a meaningful way.

"How Can I Calm My Child's Fears If I Can't Calm My Own?"

Learning to distinguish between our needs and the needs of our children has been the focus of workshops led by Donna DeMuth, a clinical social worker in Portland, Maine. DeMuth asks participants to consider the question, "How can I help my children grow up in a dangerous world?" Her workshops originally were intended for therapists who work with children and families. "But what I found," she says, "was that therapists didn't want to talk about their clinical experiences with kids. They wanted to talk about *their own kids* and *their own feelings* about dealing with the nuclear topic with their children. Sophisticated psychiatrist-types . . . bright, well-educated people were saying, 'I don't feel comfortable talking with my kids because I can't reassure them that everything will be all right.' "

Furthermore, the general public expressed greater interest in attending the workshops than therapists, something DeMuth had not expected. Although some workshop participants were active in the peace movement, "the vast majority were ordinary parents who welcomed the opportunity to struggle with their feelings and practice their responses in a safe environment—then go back and talk with their children.

"I help them sort out their feelings, right then and there in the session," DeMuth explains. "They usually express one of two basic motivations: 'I want to learn how to talk about this for my kid's sake,' or 'I have to come to grips with my own feelings before I can talk with my kids about their's.' " Some participants wanted technical information. "That's okay," DeMuth says. "Education is important. But I believe that it has to come *after* people have dealt with their emotions." She believes effective parent-child communication occurs only after the adults have begun

- to face their own fears
- to let go of the need to "make everything nice"
- to say "I don't know" gracefully
- to deal with guilt
- to acknowledge feelings of helplessness
- to become part of a larger support network
- to help children verbalize their thoughts and feelings
- to help children feel safe despite our lack of trust in the world
- to comprehend the finality of nuclear war
- to live a normal life in spite of our fears.

Although many people were discouraged when they began the program, most left "feeling activated, feeling like they wanted to do something."

In describing her workshops, DeMuth explains that a bonding of the group takes place very quickly. "The subject is so emotional that people connect much quicker than a group that talks about marital problems, self-improvement, or some other topic. People feel free to say that they are totally stumped, that they don't know how to talk to kids about nuclear war, that they're afraid of saying or doing the wrong thing. By coming to the workshops and trying to discover how other adults handle this matter, they've already taken an important step."

Role-playing is an integral part of DeMuth's workshops, and this exercise yields interesting results about the way many adults tend to talk with children about nuclear issues. In these exercises, participants are paired: one plays a child, the other plays an adult. Then they switch roles. DeMuth suggests the following situation: "You're an adult, and this is a child. This child comes to you with some concern about the world." The "child" is told to "push the adult hard, be persistent, don't settle for unsatisfactory answers."

Two things happen. "First, the adult who plays the child gets a chance to safely ventilate his or her deepest feelings," DeMuth says. "These people really pour their hearts and souls out. They have permission, being only 'six.' It's a permission they don't grant themselves as adults. Second, the person who plays the adult has to struggle with their own intuitive responses. Then, in a debriefing, the person who played the child gives them feedback about what helped and what didn't. That's very powerful."

DeMuth notes that many adults "who are normally warm and expressive *don't even think to give the kid a hug.* It's incredible! You could say that this is because people are stiff and self-conscious in role-play, but I'm really good at facilitating role-play; people get into it. It's not that. It's people's genuine, frozen response to questions from children about nuclear war.

"That's not universally true, of course," she adds. "There are those who find it easy to be comfortable and supportive of their children's problems. But a lot of adults are surprised to find out they cannot be supportive in the same way they'd normally be to a cut finger or a disappointment. Their expectations for their behavior are so high that they're frozen.

"So what they do is lecture," she says. "Over and over again, the people who played the child will give them the feedback: 'You talked too much. You tried to give me information I wasn't ready for.' Or they tried to minimize the child's fear with 'Oh, it's not that bad,' or 'Don't worry about it'—words that aren't reassuring, just mechanical."

People who played the parent are always surprised when they fail—when they don't get favorable feedback from the "children." And DeMuth finds that most adults fail. "Once you reverse roles, things get better. Now the 'parent' gets to play the 'child.' It's easier the second time. Participants have many opportunities to practice, rehearse, and learn better ways of responding to a child's questions."

DeMuth is gratified by the response to her workshops. "Almost everyone comes out with a real commitment to talk to their kids.

Those who choose not to are rare, but I encourage them to make that statement and feel honorable about it. But I do ask them to make it a *conscious* turn-off."

Developmental Concerns

In a previous book, *Crisis Counseling with Children and Adolescents*,[14] we suggested ways parents and other important adults in a child's life—grandparents, teachers, members of the clergy, scout masters, favorite neighbors—can talk to children about traumatic or stressful events. We pointed out ways these adults can communicate to children of different ages, stressed the importance of seeing the world through the child's eyes, and noted the folly of trying to impose adult logic on a child's way of thinking. Children have their own particular logic, and adults listening to and talking with a child must remember this.

Pervasive fear of nuclear war is a genuine crisis for some children. If important adults don't take the time to be with these children, answer their questions, discuss their worries, and correct their misguided thinking, then this crisis could turn them in the wrong direction and lead to more serious problems.

Some events can develop into a greater crisis for the adult than for the child. "Do I do something about this situation or not?" "What's the best way to help my child?" "What should I say?" This in particular is the case when adults are faced with a child's distress at the thought of a nuclear war.

One thing to remember when beginning a discussion with children about nuclear issues is that *children think differently than adults*.

Let's consider ways adults can talk to children of different ages and stages of emotional development about nuclear issues.

Toddlers (Birth to Three Years)

Babies and toddlers need the love and security of a home. This gives them the strength and confidence to face problems as they grow older. To suggest that they sense imminent global destruction, or that we should alert them to this possibility, is inappropriate.

Magic Years Children (Ages Three to Six)

Magic years children, as Selma Fraiberg[15] refers to them, are learning to be part of a world which is larger than their immediate family. They are immersed in discovery, wonder, play, reckless abandon, and fantasy. Yet the magic that colors their thought does not simply refer to their belief in the tooth fairy, Santa, and the Easter Bunny; it also refers to their belief that their own thoughts can influence objects and events in the world around them. They feel *responsible* for a sibling's illness if they have been mean to that sibling; for accidents that happened to others; or for parental fights or divorce. They believe that their thoughts about an event can cause it to happen.

Magic years children are beginning to control their emotions and impulses, and sometimes their feelings frighten them. Anger is particularly real because they are struggling to control it, and suggestions of violence in their environment (television, movies, scary stories, family feuds) can be extremely upsetting, often causing nightmares, because it implies that adults on whom they rely cannot control it either. Consequently, references to nuclear war can be traumatic.

It would be best if these children were allowed to grow up in relative innocence and concentrate on mastering the challenges of their environment before being burdened with "grown-up" problems. However, we can't always insulate children from the world around them. As we've noted several times, many four- and five-year-olds pick up allusions to atomic bombs from other children, television, music, video games, and comments spoken by adults. These inquisitive youngsters zero in on the negative aspects of this information and dwell on it. Adults need to acknowledge young children's concerns, to be accessible to their questions, to be perceived as someone the child can always turn to when troubled, and to assure the child that he or she is protected and loved. Most important, adults should answer young children's questions about nuclear warfare as positively and re-assuringly as possible, redirect their attention to the good things in the world, and let them know what people are doing to make the world safer.

Think twice about admitting your fears to magic years children. It may be all right to say that you worry about nuclear war in a conversation with a fifteen-year-old son or daughter; it is ill-advised to tell the same to a six-year-old. Young children need positive and reassuring messages: if adults project fear and uncertainty, the child will absorb these feelings and become distressed.

An example from World War II illustrates this point. Elizabeth Geleerd, writing in 1942 on "The Psychiatric Care of Children in Wartime," noted Anna Freud's observations of young children and their mothers during the air raids over London in the Battle of Britain. "Her reports bring out very closely that only those children showed anxiety or other disturbances whose mothers were very frightened."[16] Remarkably, these children quickly calmed down once they were separated from their panicky mothers.

Geleerd observed this first-hand when treating refugees who had fled to England from Continental battle zones. Most were families with children. Although the children had been subjected to all the stress and horrors of war, none of them showed symptoms of anxiety, shock, or nightmares. Geleerd attributed this to the fact that the children had not been separated from their families, and that "the parents had not lost their heads."[17] They had somehow managed to help their children feel safe in the madness of a warring world.

With magic years children (and older children as well), listen carefully to their questions and respond only to what is asked. "A child who asks what makes the car go does not require a treatise on the internal combustion engine. You can keep yourself out of uncomfortably deep water by *listening carefully* to the child's question and answering only what has been asked."[18] Similarly, if a four-year-old asks, "What is an atom bomb?" an answer such as, "It's a very powerful bomb that can destroy a big area and kill a lot of people" will probably satisfy the child's curiosity. It is not necessary to school the child with facts and information he or she is neither ready for nor interested in knowing.

In summary: With young children, respond to their questions and concerns about nuclear issues. If you don't, the child will get information, or misinformation, elsewhere. Listen carefully, and answer only what has been asked. Tell the truth. A well-meant lie is worse than refusing to discuss the subject at all. Keep your answers simple, direct, and as positive as possible. Young children need to feel safe, secure, and loved. Finally, remember that young children often ask the same questions repeatedly. Continue to answer them patiently: the child may not have understood you the first time, may have heard contradictory information, or may simply need further reassurance that he or she is cared about and loved.[19]

Middle Years Children (Ages Six to Twelve)

Because middle years children do not think abstractly, their reflections about death are specific and detailed. Adults might view their preoccupations as morose, macabre, and morbid, but they are normal for children of this age. For example, many six-through twelve-year-olds ask questions at wakes or funerals that adults learned to suppress long ago: "Why is Grandma so hard and cold?" or "Will the body rot in the ground?" Such questions help children master their fears.

One mother and her nine-year-old daughter visited an exhibit of art by survivors of the bombing of Nagasaki. The daughter asked, "Would my skin come off in a nuclear war like in those pictures?" The astonished mother responded in the most positive way she knew: "That's a very scary question for me to think about because I love you so much. But yes, the truth is it would . . ." and went on to explain that many people are working hard to prevent nuclear warfare.[20]

Be a good listener with middle years children and observe their nonverbal cues. Pay attention to their play, writing, and artwork. Create a climate in which they can voice their concerns, at their own pace. Don't force discussions on them, but try to find out what they're thinking. Ask questions that might help them say what's on their mind. ("Do you think about this often?") Sum things up occasionally. ("It seems you're trying to say . . ." or "Does that answer all your questions?") Remember that the truth is less frightening than mystery, and many children have misperceptions about living in a nuclear age. Answers to simple questions like, "What are atom bombs?," "How are they set off?" or "Who makes them?" may give youngsters a more realistic understanding of the matter.[21]

Middle years children, for whom school is an intimate part of their lives, may be reluctant to admit their rudimentary understanding of the nuclear problem, or avoid discussion for fear of saying "something dumb." Reassure them that nuclear issues are very complicated, and that there are no right or wrong questions.

Sometimes a question may stump you. By saying, "I don't know the answer to that one. It's a really good question; we'll have to find out," you communicate to the child that his or her concern is valid. Children rarely expect as much of adults as adults do of themselves. Learn together with your children: watch experts debate on TV, read about the subject and discuss what you've read, attend public meetings. Talk about the themes of popular movies, books, and music, and pursue education about nuclear issues through the vast variety of resources available.

Once an adult has established a relationship in which children feel free to ask whatever is on their mind, heavier themes may surface. Sometimes a question about nuclear war conceals deeper concerns. Just as questions about sex may mask musings about "Where did I come from, *really?*," factual queries about nuclear war might cloak fears and anxieties related to "How will I end?," "Is life worth living?" or "How long will we be together?"

Finally, we are not suggesting that children worry night and day about nuclear issues. They don't. The intent of this section is to offer information and advice to those adults who think nuclear weapons and nuclear war are worth discussing with children, either now or at some future time.

Talking with Teens

Penny Jaworski, Youth Activities Coordinator for the Catholic Archdiocese of Chicago, has participated in hundreds of discussions with teenagers about important issues over the years. Nuclear war is one of these issues.

It is her experience that most teenagers *don't* want to talk about nuclear war, just as most adults don't, even when they are deeply troubled by it. "It seems to me that kids today don't have a lot of hope, there's a feeling that the world isn't going to be around for them. They feel powerless, almost as if they're treading water. They don't look ahead anymore. They have less ambition to achieve. They're holding back a lot, and I think it's because other people are making decisions for them—important decisions about bombs and missiles and war."

Jaworski says that nobody likes to admit that they're afraid of something, but once rapport has been established between people, they begin to talk more openly. "I think adolescents need to hear from adults that we all have questions, we all doubt sometimes, we all wonder what's going on, and that we aren't always in control. But it would be phoney to say that nuclear war scares you if you never think about it.

"For example, when I talk with kids about alcohol, I share with them incidents about people in my life who've been hurt by it. I think the same applies to a frank discussion of feelings about nuclear war. *You have to share a real experience.* If you really do wonder, it's okay to say, 'I have questions about this,' without shaking a kid's foundation.

"Too often," she says, "teenagers look at rigid adults and mutter, 'They think they have all the answers,' then tune them out. I think you have more credibility when you share your uncertainty. I've always thought it a fallacy that adults have to be in control of everything. That's an unrealistic position, a myth about adulthood that ought to be retired. If you know something, or believe something, you should be able to say it. But if you don't, the same holds true.

"It's important to get the word out to adults that they can be themselves when they talk about nuclear war," Jaworski emphasizes. "This will enable young people to be themselves, too."

Many adults who talk with teens about nuclear weapons and war get caught up in the political debate surrounding the issues: the advisability of various weapons systems and strategies; the advantages and disadvantages of disarmament or a freeze; the ulterior motives of the superpowers who have nuclear arsenals. We usually feel more comfortable, more in control, and more intelligent when we talk on a factual level rather than an emotional one.

Although "the facts" are vitally important when talking to children of this age, as we'll discuss later, it is neither necessary nor always advisable to begin a dialog on nuclear issues from a political context. Merely asking exploratory questions such as, "What do you think about the nuclear arms buildup?" or "How does all this talk about nuclear war affect you?" offers teens an opportunity to voice their opinions, ask other questions, learn how their peers feel, and examine what they can do in helping find a solution to the problem.

Peace Education

Much of the material that is part of the "peace education" curricula in some schools has·been roundly criticized. In fact, President Reagan chastised the National Education Association for "frightening and brainwashing American schoolchildren"[22] with its material prepared for junior-high students. Other critics, including parents, teachers, and politicians, maintain that most peace studies programs are more indoctrination than education. They feel these courses have too much of a pro-disarmament bias, with not enough attention given to opposing points of view.

Acknowledging the various thoughts, feelings, and opinions of individuals within a group can be managed, but how do we handle the political tinderbox the nuclear issue has become? How do we lead a balanced, objective discussion in a group where some members are adamantly committed to nuclear disarmament and others just as stubbornly dedicated to the doctrine of nuclear deterrence?

Jaworski has faced this situation many times. Her recommendation: "In any class, group, or individual discussion, you have to ask teens to listen to both sides, and you need to model this ability for them." She emphasizes that everyone needs facts on which to base an opinion.

"Sometimes we base our decisions on emotions. This is okay, but we have to know when we're doing it. We need to be able to say to ourselves, 'This is not a logical position. I'm basing it on my feelings.' And if I'm doing this, I have to respect the decisions of others who are doing the same thing."

Jaworski counsels everyone: *Get the facts.* "If I'm called upon to make a serious decision, a commitment about something important, my decision should be based not only on feelings, but on facts," she says. "We have to consider both sides. Often, with controversial subjects like drugs or alcohol or abortion or nuclear arms, we try to show others how 'horrible' the opposing side is. A better way—especially when you work with kids—is to help them make informed decisions based not just on their feelings, but on the facts and values presented by opposing sides.

"I encourage kids to respect other people's opinions, but also to evaluate if others have checked their facts. Encourage them to read things that disagree with their viewpoint so that they can make solid, informed decisions."

Allowing Young People to Make Their Own Decisions

One of the biggest responsibilities of parenthood is preparing children for the future. We must encourage them to think critically, to think for themselves, and to learn to make their own decisions.

Sometimes we forget that children learn by example. They adopt many of our tastes, habits, faults, and virtues. They pick up the good with the bad, and they frequently acquire our thinking and attitudes about many matters, big and small. This includes politics.

However, with an issue as complex and controversial as nuclear war, we would be negligent in our responsibilities if we didn't point out that there is a divergence of opinions and many different, valid, persuasive arguments on all sides. When we explain: "Not everybody feels like Mom and Pop," we instill in children a respect for other opinions and give them the latitude to come to their own conclusions on nuclear issues.

James W. Douglass, a university professor turned full-time peace activist respected for his nonviolent approach to the nuclear problem, emphasizes the importance of allowing his twelve-year-old son, Thomas, the freedom to decide for himself what activities he'll participate in with his parents. Douglass strongly believes that "drafting" his son into peace activities against his wishes would be a form of violence, and could motivate him to turn his life in another direction. He feels that it's a "natural phenomenon" for children of parents involved in the peace movement to adopt an opposite stance, such as joining the military. Acknowledging the possibility that his son "may end up enlisting in the U.S. Navy," he notes that parents in the military sometimes discover their kids joining the peace movement.

While Douglass says the expression of one's own adult commitment is vital, "if parents in either area can give their kids the freedom they need, then those kids will make a decision that appears most responsible to them and is not just a rebellion against the parents."

Many people, teens and adults alike, are firmly committed to a particular position on the nuclear arms issue. In group discussions, they often become obsessed with trying to get their point across while struggling to convince another to change his or her opinion. This didactic approach does little to encourage others in the group to probe deeper into the matter for themselves. Striving to be open and receptive to differing opinions (and helping others to do the same) will result in more meaningful and constructive dialog.

Roberta Snow, president of Educators for Social Responsibility and coordinator of a high-school curriculum project entitled, "Decision Making in a Nuclear Age: Confronting Nuclear Weapons," says the goals of this program are "to educate students about the arms race and the issues of responsibility, and to give them different perspectives on it. The key is to help them become socially responsible for the world they live in."

Snow said that when ESR was first formed, "Somebody said to us, 'Well, I understand why the doctors are organizing, because it's a medical issue. And I understand why the lawyers are organizing, because it's about negotiations. But why are the teachers organizing?' That's really an enormous statement about the devaluing of education."[23]

Rutgers professor Milton Schwebel puts it another way. "Anyone acquainted with the history of the American school since World War II can genuinely sympathize with the argument that we've dumped on schools every conceivable social problem, reduced the time available for the established curriculae, and then blamed them for the declining student performance. We can hardly expect the schools to solve the problems of the nuclear threat. However, this topic is not some unrelated extra. It *is* the curriculum; it's science and history, literature and economics and drama. It's their life experience, a source of relevance and motivation for students."[24]

Another question Snow is frequently asked: "How do we talk to children about nuclear weapons?" She thinks the question itself is the problem. "Maybe it should be, 'How do we *listen* to children when they talk about nuclear weapons?' And how do we prepare them to live in a real democracy by caring about how they think? Not just caring about how they think about the social problems that are important to them, but by helping them understand that the problems we're facing now are not just about nuclear weapons. It's about teaching people to be socially active in the world— to take risks, to find the courage to stand up for what they believe in." She says that perhaps the greatest sign of hope is that students are *demanding* that adults do something. At the end of a pilot course on "Decision Making in a Nuclear Age," a ninth-grade boy observed, "You know, this course could be dangerous. Because if you put it in every school in the country, and kids take it seriously, that lets adults off the hook."[25]

Snow is adamant: "We have to remind them, and remind our-selves, that adults are *not* off the hook. By talking to our kids or by teaching peace courses in classrooms, we aren't shirking our responsibility. We need to provide them with role models who take this issue seriously, and let them know that we're not enlisting them in the political campaigns of adults. That's our battle. The nuclear weapons freeze is not a student movement. But students have their own ways of confronting the problem, their own things they can do about it, their own ways they can think about it. We need to support them in those efforts. I think we probably give children the greatest hope when we can look them straight in the eye and say, 'I am doing everything I can to prevent nuclear war.' We're caring for them by making the world safer."[26]

Not everyone agrees with Snow. The integration of peace cur-ricula into a growing number of schools across the country has become a hotbed of controversy among teachers, administrators, and parents. Not only do many parents object to study units on nuclear war at the expense of time spent on the mastery of primary knowledge and skills, they also suspect these courses are designed to change attitudes and behavior, "to promote U.S. nuclear dis-armament, to belittle the Soviet threat, and to propagandize for federal spending for social goals at the expense of national de-fense."[27] They resent teaching techniques that ask students to bare their private thoughts and worries; they are upset by text-books, films, and other materials which may arouse feelings of fear, guilt, and despair; and they are angered by what they see as classroom attempts to brainwash children with social values or political viewpoints different from ones many families hold.

Yet *London Times* education correspondent Lucy Hodges writes: "If children are to learn about war and peace, how to prevent the former and preserve the latter, there needs to be cool dis-cussion about what goes into the course. And just because it is called peace studies it need not mean (as some suggest) that it has to be about 'appeasement and surrender to any totalitarian forces threatening our society.' "

Robert Sperber, superintendent, Brookline, Massachusetts Public

Schools, concurs. "My own sense as an educator tells me that if a subject is avoided, if it is too controversial, then that is all the more reason why it should be included in the experiences of learners. As educators, we have a responsibility to deal with controversy, for it is out of conflict and disequilibrium that real learning takes place. We cannot allow others to take away our right to think critically."

Educators, he feels, "have a responsibility to teach students content about nuclear issues, to help them make intelligent choices, to help them think about a critical issue and to give them a useful outlet for their thoughts and their feelings."

Support for these programs is mounting in the wake of several statements by church leaders, particularly the U.S. Catholic bishops. The Most Reverend Howard J. Hubbard, Bishop of Albany, New York, sees their value, yet believes it is absolutely essential that there be close communication between home and school so that parents know what their children are learning. "We cannot work with schoolchildren in a vacuum," he stresses. "Whatever message we communicate to the children we must also communicate to the parents, because they are still going to be the prime educators."

Without adequate home-school communication, studies about nuclear issues could be self-defeating and lead to serious problems. "If kids are getting contradictory messages at home," he explains, "or if parents don't understand what is being taught in the schools, or if kids come home and report what they've learned to parents who react angrily without any understanding of what the teacher meant—or disagree with it entirely—then I think this will create further fears and polarization between parents and children. What will probably happen is that the kids won't come home and discuss it any further, but they'll still have all this turmoil locked inside them.

"I think with an issue this volatile, it's very important that parents be exposed to what will be presented to their children. They must have an opportunity to discuss this among themselves and to come to some consensus in their own minds as to where they stand on the issue."

Hubbard believes that these discussions cannot take place on an intellectual level only. "You have to give people an opportunity to vent their emotions, because this is an emotional as well as an intellectual thing." He acknowledges that there is likely to be a divergence of opinion *within the schools themselves* among teachers who react to the study of peace and war in general. To assist teachers in clarifying their views, his diocese is conducting workshops on this issue to encourage open communication, respect for different opinions, and a feeling of common purpose. "I think the same thing has to be done with parents and family members if there is going to be any effective communication between them and their children on this issue."

Respecting Other Viewpoints

Throughout this book, one of our most difficult tasks was striving for balance—presenting material that could be useful to people with different political opinions. Whether adults are politically conservative, middle-of-the-road, or liberal, whether they favor strong nuclear deterrence or are violently opposed to it, they all have one paramount goal in common: the protection and security of their family and their country. It follows that people of opposing political views are also loving and concerned adults who attempt to address children's fears in a manner that they feel is constructive, reassuring, and psychologically healthy.

The split of opinion over how best to protect ourselves militarily and yet remain true to the pacifist teachings of our churches is an area of concern for Bishop Hubbard. As vicar of a diocese that includes the capital of New York State as well as a rural area stretching across fourteen counties, his responsibility is to "shepherd a flock" of intelligent, sincere adults from wide-ranging social, economic, and political backgrounds. His dilemma—and the dilemma of all who believe that they know best how to work for peace—is how to express deeply held convictions without alienating those who happen to think and feel differently.

Regardless of our particular political viewpoint, "there is a kind of stirring within the soul of humanity itself to react against this collision course to a worldwide holocaust that I think we're on,"

Hubbard commented. "That stirring is going to cross ideological spectrums, and is probably going to exist on both sides of the Iron Curtain. I believe there is a survival instinct common to all humanity, and I think this instinct is moving to the fore."

With regard to the Catholic bishops' statement on war and peace, Hubbard points out that even though this document rejects certain actions like nuclear first strike, one can read it and come to different conclusions. While the pastoral letter is far from vague, it purposely addresses the nuclear arms issue in language that recognizes that the problem is viewed in many ways. He also emphasized the importance of understanding and respecting different political viewpoints, and of keeping channels of communication open between people committed to opposite solutions to the nuclear crisis.

Within his diocese, Hubbard finds three basic responses to the nuclear threat. "One group—and they tend to be a very vocal group—is frightened by the prospect of nuclear war; they work for anything they believe will put an end to the entire munitions industry in this country and thereby bring about cessation of warfare as a way of resolving disputes between nations.

"There's another group," he continued, "that I think just doesn't see the issue at all. They more or less don't understand what it's about, and really don't want to hear about it.

"The third group, and I think this is the largest group, is concerned about the problem and understands, to a certain extent, the issues involved. But they also have a great fear about 'What happens if we give up our nuclear weapons? What happens if we stop our research and development programs? What happens if we begin to disarm unilaterally?' They sincerely believe there *is* an international communist conspiracy. They believe that the Soviet Union and its allies are not honorable. They see what happened in Afghanistan. They see what happened in Poland. They take a look at what's happened historically to weaker nations who've been preyed upon by stronger nations," he said. Their motivation, although often not articulated, is similar psychologically to that of the first group. "These people have a great fear.

They're saying, 'If we pursue this to the logical conclusion, but only do it unilaterally, and the Russians don't seem to be open to dialog about it, is our latter state going to be worse than our former?' For them," Hubbard said, "it comes down to the age-old question, 'Are we better Red than dead, or dead than Red?'

"I remember when Father Bryan Hehir, one of the chief drafters of the bishops' statement, lectured here several years ago. He tried to outline in detail the rationale for the pastoral letter. There was a lively discussion, mostly favorable, along the general lines the document eventually took. Yet there was one woman at the end who said, 'I'm the mother of three children, and as I listen to you, I want to say, "Amen!" and "Yes!" to everything you are saying. But when I read the newspaper or watch the evening news [this was about the time the Russians invaded Afghanistan] I get frightened, and my fear overcomes what I hear you saying.' "

Hubbard gave another example of when those dedicating themselves to peace provoked the ire of veteran's groups within the diocese. "We held a prayer service to commemorate the bombing of Hiroshima. The message was, 'To remember Hiroshima is to avoid nuclear war. To remember Hiroshima is to commit oneself to peace.' And the bishops' pastoral letter itself says that unless we can experience sorrow for what happened at Hiroshima, it will be very difficult for us to find the strength and determination to reverse the arms race."

Although many were inspired by this pledge, others were angered, Hubbard remembered. "You get responses from war veterans who say: 'If it weren't for the atom bomb, I might have been killed in World War II. I was a serviceman at that time, and many of my friends and relatives had already died in the war. As far as I'm concerned, nuclear bombs aren't the evil you're portraying them as. Japan started the war, and this was just desserts for their aggression. I don't feel sorrow for it. I don't feel repentance for it. I think that we're naive if we give up weapons of this nature.' "

Hubbard is convinced that "a strong feeling like this exists out there. We have to deal with people's real fears about 'How do nations defend themselves against those who have different ideals and different values?' I don't know if we have the answer to that, but unless we recognize the fears that people have, it will be very difficult to talk to adults or children about this issue."

DILEMMAS AND DIALOGS

Now we'll look at some common themes which emerge when adults and young people attempt to discuss nuclear issues with one another. In the following pages, we present a series of exercises, "Dilemmas and Dialogs." Some of these are accompanied by a brief commentary; others are not, setting the stage for further thought and consideration on the reader's part.

1. *"Do we bring it up, or wait until they do?"* This dilemma troubles adults, especially those with young children. Statistics show that over 40 percent of the children in this country come from broken homes. More than 90 percent of high-schoolers have experienced the death of a relative or friend. Nuclear war? Why expose children to even more pain and uncertainty? We know how easily children's fears can be stirred up. (How many parents have told their seven- or eight-year-olds a scary bedtime story, only to be awakened later when the youngster climbs into bed with them for reassurance and safety?) The experts caution us not to expose children to the grisly details of a nuclear war at too early an age. Warns Dr. John Dunne, a child psychiatrist: "Six- and seven-year-olds can be 'shaken up' by improperly handled discussions, and even ten- to twelve-year-olds have trouble with the subject because in their pre-puberty stage their emotions are already close to the surface."[28]

Nevertheless, we also know children pick up bits and pieces of information about nuclear arms from television, magazines, music, school, other kids, and grown-ups' remarks. They hear about it even when we think they don't.

> *Dilemma:* It is a weekday evening, and the family is gathered in the TV room, watching a wildlife program. A newsbreak comes on, and the commentator announces: "Special report on the nuclear arms race. Details at eleven." The parents and

their three children—ages eight, twelve, and fifteen—remain silent, waiting for the wildlife program to resume. Their faces are inscrutable. But the parents wonder what the kids are thinking. Are they worried about a war? Do they have an optimistic outlook for the future? Should we bring up the issue, or wait until they do?

2. *"Put it out of your mind."* In general, dwelling on the negative is not a healthy human response to life. Is this the best attitude to adopt toward the nuclear issue?

Dialog: A sixteen-year-old boy is sprawled across the living room sofa, reading a national news magazine. The cover story is on the nuclear arms race. The boy's father is seated in an overstuffed chair, reading a newspaper.

BOY: Dad, do you worry about nuclear war?
DAD: Not really. I think it's best just to put it out of your mind.

3. *Acknowledging negative feelings.* Some adults think that talking about unpleasant facts in the home will make a bad situation worse. They fear that giving attention to a problem reinforces it—that taking notice of a child's anger will cause further outbursts, that mentioning a child's fears or worries will provoke anxiety. This is unfortunate because the *avoidance* of dealing with a child's emotions sometimes is what intensifies them, not the act of discussing them. If done properly, talking about feelings helps a child come to grips with them and feel less isolated.

Note these dialogs. In the second, both people feel stronger and closer because the truth of the situation was acknowledged.

Dialog A: A teenager comes home and joins his parents at the dinner table. He has managed to squeeze in an hour at home between football practice and a night in the library.

TEENAGER: It really irks me when I think about the kind of world that has been handed down to us. We could die any minute!
PARENT: Yeah, but there's nothing we can do about it. It's best not to dwell on it. Want to go to the movies tonight after you study?

Dialog B:

PARENT: (responding to above angry statement by teenager) You sound so angry! What's on your mind?

TEENAGER: We had a guest lecturer in class today. It's incredible—there're over 50,000 atomic bombs in the world! And the U.S. keeps building more! It's sick!

PARENT: It is horrible and frightening and unfair. Most adults don't seem to be able to face it, let alone solve it. They turn their attention to other problems.

TEENAGER: What have you tried to do?

PARENT: It's a difficult thing for me to face up to. I get angry, too, when I think about it. I read up on it and vote for people I think will keep us out of war. But sometimes I just need to put it out of my mind.

TEENAGER: Yeah—you'd go crazy if you thought about it all the time

PARENT: Maybe after your studies tonight, we can go to a movie? You up for that?

4. *Admitting mixed feelings.* Almost everyone has mixed feelings about nuclear issues, and the unique blend of these feelings varies from person to person. A career military officer will feel differently about them than will a Quaker minister. People with opposing political or ideological viewpoints often avoid topical discussions because these tend to balloon into heated disagreements. An honest admission of the feelings that underlie a political or religious stance is one way to improve communication.

Dialog: Fifteen-year-old Kate is helping her dad wax the car. Kate's father is an electronics engineer who has recently been assigned to work on a guidance system for nuclear missiles. Kate has been active in a nuclear freeze movement in the community, and plans to take a bus to a rally in Washington. Kate cautiously asks her dad about his new assignment.

KATE: Dad, you like your new job?

FATHER: I like the technical part of it—it'll be a real challenge. I'm not too thrilled about how it's going to be placed on a nuclear missile to guide it to its target.

KATE: I thought you were for nukes.

FATHER: Now that's a loaded question. If it were up to me, I'd throw out every missile—here, Russia, France, India, wherever. But the arms buildup has gone so far that we need to have a defense. Sometimes I'd like to speak out . . . but I'm only six years away from my pension. That means a lot to your mom and me.

KATE: You're sort of trapped?

FATHER: You might say that. I wish it were a different world, but I have a responsibility to our family. When's your next meeting on the freeze?

KATE: Next Tuesday. We can't vote yet, but we think the politicians will listen to us if there's enough of us. Someone's got to take a stand on this.

FATHER: You're doing your best to make a difference.

5. *"I-statements" on nuclear issues.* One way to achieve effective communication with teens and provide them with a good role model is to preface your opinions with "I-statements." People who say, " I think . . . ," " It's my opinion that . . . ," or countless variations thereof are generally better communicators on emotionally charged topics than those who make judgmental remarks ("It's wrong . . ." or "The only way . . .") or ask rhetorical questions ("Who has the answer?").

In addition, I-statements are less likely to provoke resistance and rebellion from teens. To let adolescents know that you *do* have an opinion, you *do* think about nuclear issues, and that you *aren't* overwhelmed with a sense of helplessness and hopelessness is good.

Consider the effectiveness of the following examples. Which speaker is more open to the other person's point of view?

ADULT A: I'm fearful for our country's safety. I've lived through three wars and it seems to me that weak nations are always taken advantage of by stronger ones. I'd like to see this country continue to develop a strong defense. Nuclear weapons scare me but, unfortunately, I'm afraid they're here to stay. If we don't have them, I think we put ourselves at the mercy of those who do.

ADULT B: Nuclear weapons are wrong and crazy and it's time everyone did something to stop them. An immediate freeze followed by disarmament is the only rational course for thinking people. Those arguments about a strong national defense are absurd.

6. *Providing factual information.* Children and teenagers are often confused about nuclear issues and need information or clarification from adults. The tone set by the adult helps direct the course of the conversation. What do you think will be the result of the following conversations?

Dialog A: Father and son are watching the network evening news, which includes reports from West Germany and Britain on the massive protests against installing cruise and Pershing II missiles in those countries. Seventeen-year-old Jeffrey, who has read a lot about the European perspective on nuclear arms, watches the reports with keen interest.

JEFFREY: Hey, Dad, what do you think about those people in Europe who don't want NATO missiles?

DAD: Aw, those Europeans are a bunch of nuts. They want the U.S. to protect them, but they don't want to pay the price. The communists are behind all those protests.

JEFFREY: But Dad, the reporter says most people over there don't like being caught in the middle of a problem they see as a quarrel between the U.S. and Russia. They say they're tired of war, and don't want the U.S. and Russia to fight their nuclear battles in their countries. I can understand that.

DAD: I can't. I don't want nuclear bombs falling on America. Those Europeans should have thought about that before they started World War II.

Dialog B: Fourteen-year-old Penny is riding the bus to her violin lesson. The two passengers seated behind her are college students discussing the nuclear freeze issue. Penny listens intently to what they are saying. She's almost sorry when they get off the bus. It's the first time she's heard about nuclear war in a way that helped her understand some of the issues. She thinks about this discussion throughout her lesson, and brings it up with her teacher after class.

PENNY: Mr. Williams, what's a nuclear freeze?

TEACHER: That's something a lot of people have been concerned about lately. Bare bones, it means that we would talk to the Russians, and they would talk to us, and both countries would agree not to build any more atomic bombs or missiles. Of course, it's more complicated. . . . Can you think of other questions you might want to ask? Maybe we could both try to understand this a little better.

Dialog C: It's 9:30 P.M., and the fire siren in a small Midwestern town goes off. Josh, who is six years old, looks at his mother worriedly.

JOSH: Mom, do you think that could be the Bomb?
MOTHER: It sounds like the fire siren, honey. It's a scary thought, though, isn't it? It seems a lot of people have been thinking about that lately. It's always in the news. What do you know about it, honey? Do your friends talk about it? Are you worried?

Dialog D: Energy resources and conservation are being studied in ten-year-old Rita's science class. Rita has been assigned to give a report on nuclear energy. She's confused and worried, and mentions it to her parents that evening.

RITA: Nuclear energy is bad, isn't it? Don't nuclear power plants hurt the earth? Can't they blow up?
DAD: If something goes wrong, sure. They can hurt people, too. There's a risk involved. There are pros and cons. Let's go into the den and talk about it. And let's check the encyclopedia. (. . . Goes on to talk about Einstein and atoms, how atomic bombs are different from atomic energy, using simple language and analogies, drawing out Rita's questions.)

7. *Acknowledging feelings of helplessness.* All adults, from time to time, feel helpless when they think about the complexity of the nuclear question. This is a universal response. In the following example, Karen's mother is honest about her fears. This genuine sharing of feelings helps Karen feel less isolated.

Dialog: Sixteen-year-old Karen is lying on her bed, staring at the ceiling. Her bedroom door is closed, and her stereo is playing. She is moody and depressed because of a discussion on nuclear war in that day's sociology class. The song she is listening to has haunting lyrics: ". . . dust in the wind, all we are is dust in the wind." At dinner that evening, she is quiet and sullen.

MOTHER: How's everything?
KAREN: (shrugs)
MOTHER: (talks about her day)
KAREN: This morning, in sociology, we discussed nuclear war. I'm so bummed out. It's so confusing. It's so complicated. Each side has a point. But you can't help but feel there's gonna be a war anyway.
MOTHER: I feel the same way when I read the papers or listen to some of those speeches on TV. Even the experts can't agree. It's sad.
KAREN: Yeah, that's the worst part. It seems that so little is being done to prevent it.

8. *Signs of trouble.* Although the nuclear issue is a genuine problem in its own right, sometimes we complain about it when something totally unrelated troubles us. Therapists call this displacement—directing worry or concern to an area of life that isn't worthy of so much emotional investment and is not the real source of our problem. In the following example, do you think Paul's immediate need is to talk about nuclear war, or to deal with the other problems in his life? What should the coach say?

Dilemma: Seventeen-year-old Paul has been angry and depressed for months. He wants to go to a top-notch college, but it looks as if his grades aren't good enough, and he scored poorly on the SAT. His father has been laid off, and there's pressure on Paul to work more hours on his after-school job. On top of all this, his girlfriend recently broke up with him. One day, after playing a poor game, he confides to his basketball coach, "With all this talk of nuclear war going on, it's hard to get through the day sometimes."

9. *Changing the world.* Many adults have set opinions about nuclear issues. In the next examples, the parents have firm, committed—but opposite—positions on the issue. Does it seem that their children have any choice but to agree with them? Are the

adults caricatures, or do you think some parents come across like this to young people?

> *Adult A:* Fifteen-year-old Sally and her twelve-year-old brother, Mark, are eating lunch in the kitchen. They are listening to their mother talk on the phone to the head of a women's church group that is planning a peace prayer vigil. They hear their mother talk passionately about peace, joy, love, and cooperation. . . .
>
> "Poor, sweet Mom," Sally says between bites of her sandwich. "She really thinks she can change the world."
>
> "Yeah," sighs Mark, rolling his eyes. "It's kinda sad."
>
> *Adult B:* Thirteen-year-old Alan has just come home from a youth group meeting held after church one Sunday. His father is sitting on the patio, sipping a beer and admiring the freshly mown lawn. Alan pulls up a chair next to his father. Peace and nuclear war was the topic of his youth group meeting.
>
> ALAN: What do you think of the Russians, Dad? Do you think they'll ever use nuclear weapons?
> FATHER: Can't trust 'em. A nation of atheists and killers. Look what those commie bastards did to those poor people on that Korean airplane. We should have nuked 'em after that.
> ALAN: What about the letter from the bishops at church? They said we all need to work for peace, that everyone on this planet is part of the people of God.
> FATHER: Right—turn the other cheek and get shot in the back! The best defense has always been a strong offense.
> ALAN: But it's morally wrong! It's insane! It's going to end up where everyone gets killed!
> FATHER: The Church should keep out of this. I've lived through two wars. Wait until you've been around as long. You'll see where idealism gets people.
> MOTHER: Time to eat!

10. *Protecting your children.* Perhaps you can think of alternative ways of handling this discussion.

> *Dilemma:* A small child, about five, is watching a television broadcast of the first hydrogen bomb testing in the desert,

and scenes of Hiroshima and Nagasaki—charred victims, burned survivors, and terrified people describing the fire flash.

CHILD: Mommy? The news says a war is coming. Are we going to die from a bomb? Are we gonna burn up, too?

MOTHER: (impatiently) Don't be silly. Those are old pictures. That happened a long time ago. There's no war coming. Go turn the news off.

CHILD: But the TV said those people were hurt real bad.

MOTHER: That was a war that happened forty years ago. I want you to forget it and think about good things. Why don't you put your shoes on and we'll go to the store.

11. *Self-disclosure.* Adults who reveal what helps them cope, not in a self-righteous manner but in a gentle, compassionate way that suggests their own struggle, offer one of the most effective means of transmitting hope.

Dialog: A ten-year-old girl is helping her mother fold laundry. She is laughing at how small her baby brother's T-shirts are compared to her father's. Her mother comments about the girl having her own family someday.

DAUGHTER: I'm not going to have kids. The world is too horrible a place to bring children into. Besides, we'll all be dead from a nuclear war.

MOTHER: (startled) Has that been on your mind lately?

DAUGHTER: Off and on. I saw a picture of a nuclear blast on TV. And I hear so much talk about how there's going to be a war 'cause that's just human nature. I don't see any reason to have kids if we're all gonna die. It would be wrong.

MOTHER: Mmmm . . . All those things you say are true, honey. They are very real worries, and almost everyone feels like that from time to time, and there's nothing we can do to make the hurts and ugliness in the world disappear. They'll always be there. That's what life is all about—facing our problems and growing stronger from facing them. I remember when you were little, and your father went off to Vietnam. . . . We didn't know if he'd ever come home again, but we went ahead with our plans. And when Uncle Jimmy died of cancer, we all felt so sad and helpless. But life has so much more beauty than ugliness. What do you think?

·5·

$\vdash\!\!\!-\!\!\!-\!\!\!-\!\!\!-\!\!\!-\!\!\!-\!\!\!\dashv$

From Despair to Hope

It may seem inconsistent to follow four chapters on talking to children about nuclear war with one about religion and nuclear war. Why the abrupt change?

Religion is a major part of the lives of many who will read this book. Many of these readers have only recently become acquainted with the seriousness of nuclear war through various pronouncements of their church leaders. (As noted in our opening chapter, virtually every major religious body in America—Catholic, Protestant, and Jewish—has taken a stand on nuclear arms.) For example, millions of U.S. Catholics in 1983 were told by their bishops that the presence of nuclear weapons creates a moral dilemma which all Catholics must address. To many people of faith, such a mandate comes as a bolt from the blue.

Religious discussions about nuclear issues generally stress choices and constructive advice on how to work for peace. They don't, however, usually examine the very real human emotions that the topic evokes in both adults and children. Since we all have differing political and ethical views on the subject, an understanding of these emotions can serve as a bridge, a common ground of sorts, for people who want to accept their churches' instructions but would rather avoid the issue entirely.

Therefore, it seems useful to look at psychological responses that occur when nuclear war is discussed. If religious adults can better understand these reactions—despair, uncertainty, optimism, hope, community—then they will be better prepared to talk with children about nuclear war.

Understanding Despair

In 1974, anthropology professor Ernest Becker was posthumously awarded a Pulitzer Prize for his book, *The Denial of Death*. A central theme of this work is that people—at all costs and in countless ways—want to avoid being conscious of death. Becker believed denying death cripples people emotionally, because by refusing to recognize death, which is so much a part of life, they blind themselves to much of life's beauty and remove themselves from a range of sensitivity and vulnerability within themselves. In fact, while Freud believed that the denial of sex led to a variety of personality difficulties, Becker believed that the denial of death was an even greater contributor to personal and cultural malaise.

Becker wrote that death, including violent and sudden death through nuclear war, needs to be faced in order for us to become more aware of life. He strongly believed that religious faith best equips us to do this. The symbols and ceremonies of most major religions focus on life-events: birth, entry into adulthood, marriage, parenting, aging, and death. Organized religion gives us a framework, a language in which to communicate these experiences to one another in community.

Becker noted that even with a healthy psychological outlook and deep religious faith, death is difficult for most of us to face. And he was speaking of "plain ol' death," not the cataclysm assured us through nuclear war. In many of us, religious faith and human doubt coexist as we struggle to come to grips with the predicaments posed by the nuclear age. The possibility of nuclear annihilation stirs negative feelings of such intensity that many religious people find it difficult to reconcile these emotions with the traditional teachings of their faith.

Despair is an emotion difficult for everyone, particularly people of faith, to come to terms with. Joanna Rogers Macy, a writer and lecturer on comparative religion, has been involved in "despair work" in numerous settings. She helps individuals label their despair, accept it as a real and natural part of their lives, and learn to use it constructively. In "How to Deal with Despair,"[1] she explains how her work applies to the buildup of nuclear weapons.

Our times bombard us with signals of distress, Macy says: "As a society, we are caught between a sense of impending apocalypse and an inability to acknowledge it."[2] When political activists, religious leaders, and other social reformers confront us with our apathy, their chastisement generally fails to move us. Our real problem is not indifference, it is dread: we are afraid to face that sense of helplessness and hopelessness that pervades our lives.

Particularly in Christianity, despair is not acceptable. It is one of the cardinal sins. In its extreme form it is the unforgivable sin, the sin against the Holy Spirit, the sin against hope. Whether it is a subliminal reaction too deep or too elusive to fathom, or an embarrassment over trespassing against those who counsel "positive thinking," many religious people recoil from an honest look at despair. They view it as a lapse of faith, a major slippage that is inconsistent with their religious beliefs.

Macy tells of an incident that occurred at a peace vigil held in a church at which Daniel Berrigan spoke of "the necessity of hope to carry us through."[3] The audience was building an emotional crescendo, and the occasional sour note of an honest, individual response—the voice of someone hurting—was not appreciated. One young man spoke up falteringly and admitted his lack of hope, even though he was committed to working for peace. His fear that he would be misunderstood or viewed as a weak person was confirmed: His genuine expression of despair was not respected by some members of the audience.

Sometimes young people are more open and honest about their feelings than adults. One fourteen-year-old, during a conversation with adults about nuclear war and the future, blurted out: "I don't pray to God because I'm not sure if I believe in God. I think and

I hope. But I don't pray because I think if there was some God present among us, among the world, the things that are happening would not be happening. If God created this world, look around! If God created this world—He, She, It—I'd fire It!"

The suppression of despair, like the suppression of any strong emotion, has its price. Macy suggests that when we try to banish our despair with "injections of optimism," our other emotional responses to the world become muted, blunted, even deadened. So what do we do with our despair? "Like grief, it must be worked through. It must be named and validated as a healthy, normal, human response to the planetary situation. Faced and experienced, despair can be *used:* as the psyche's defenses drop away, new energies are released."[4]

In the New Testament, we might infer that Christ himself experienced despair when he contemplated his future during forty days of solitude in the desert. And all of us instinctively understand the anguish behind the words, "My God, my God, why have you forsaken me?" because all of us have wondered the same at some time in our lives.

Despair is an acknowledgment of human limitations, the sad realization that our dreams may not come true, the painful awareness that we are not all-powerful and cannot shape the world according to our wants and wishes. It differs from psychological depressions (where sadness of mood affects activities and interests), or the nihilism which seems to run in cycles, particularly among college students, as a fad philosophy.

The nuclear threat is real, and one human response to this threat is despair: "the loss of the assumption that the species will inevitably pull through. It represents a genuine accession to the possibility that this planetary 'experiment' may fail. At the prospect of the extinction of our civilization, feelings of grief and horror are natural. We tend to hide them, though, from ourselves and from each other."[5]

Some people are afraid to acknowledge their despair for fear that it is a final state of mind, a rock-bottom depth from which they will never recover. Macy stresses that despair is a point along a continuum; it is a part of a natural process that leads to hope.

"For all the discomfort, there is a healing in such openness, for ourselves and perhaps the world. Opening to our despair opens us also to the love that is with us, for it is in deep caring that our anguish is rooted."[6]

Perhaps much of the intimate aspects of despair should be worked out in private, or shared with close friends. Religious ceremonies and symbols will help, but each individual must tackle this problem in his or her own way.

One nagging question: Is it appropriate to·involve children in the adult expression of despair? How much of an adult's or teen-ager's struggle with the "dark night of the soul" is appropriate for children to witness? Sorting out feelings of despair may be something best kept on an adult level. When we consider that Christ went alone into the desert for forty days, was part of this retreat so that he could endure his agony in private?

True courage often requires that we face difficult times alone and work through our problems in private, without wearing them on our sleeve for the world to see. And as parents we must remember that a child's cognitive ability may not be advanced enough to see that despair can lead to hope. When a child sees a distraught adult struggling with feelings of despair, his or her own fears are greatly amplified. Despair is something for adults to resolve in private, or with other adults. It is not an occasion to burden children with grown-up sorrow, or turn to them for encouragement and support.

In *The Clowns of God,* novelist Morris West tells how one man of faith wrestled with his ambivalence and despair over his fear of a nuclear Armageddon, and how his anguish awakened in himself and others a deep sense of oneness with humanity. As Pope, Jean Barette had a vision of an atomic holocaust. When his cardinals tried to portray him to the world as insane, he re-signed. To carry his message to the world, Barette adopted the pen-name "Johnny the Clown," and addressed his despair through a series of public letters to his Maker.

> Dear God,
> I love this funny world; but I have just heard the news that You are going to destroy it; or, worse still, You are going to sit

up in heaven and watch us destroy it, like comedians wrecking a grand piano, on which great masters have played Beethoven.

I can't argue with what You do. It's Your universe. You juggle the stars and manage to keep them all in space. But please, before the last big bang, could You explain some things to me? I know this is only one tiny planet; but it's where I live and, before I leave it, I'd like to understand it a little better. I'd like to understand You, too—as far as You'll let me—but for Johny the Clown, You'll have to make it all very simple.

. . . I've never really got it clear in my mind where You fit in. No disrespect, truly! But You see, in the circus where I work, there's an audience and there's us, the people who do the tricks, and there are the animals, too. You can't leave them out because we depend on them and they on us.

Now, the audience is wonderful. Most times they're so happy and innocent you can feel the joy coming out from them; but sometimes you can smell the cruelty, too, as if they want the tigers to attack the tamer, or the aerialist to fall from the high trapeze. So I can't really believe You're the audience!

Then there's us, the performers. We're a mixed bunch: clowns like me, acrobats, pretty girls on horseback, the people on the high wire, the women with the performing dogs and the elephants and the lions and—oh, all of it! We're a grotesque lot, really: good-hearted, yes, but sometimes crazy enough to murder each other. I could tell You tales . . . but then You know, don't You? You know us like the potter knows the vase that he's turned on his own wheel.

Some people say You're the owner of the circus and that You set up the whole show for Your own private pleasure. I could accept that. I like being a clown. I get as much fun as I give. But I can't understand why the owner would want to cut the ropes of the big top and bury us all underneath it. A mad person might do that, a vengeful villain. I don't believe You can be mad and make a rose, or vengeful and create a dolphin. . . . So You see, there is a lot of explaining to do . . .[7]

In this fictitious story, people were stirred by these simple letters because the author dared to put their own doubts and fears into words. There is also an intimate tone to the letters which implies the author's belief and trust in a caring Maker.

The U.S. Catholic bishops, in placing nuclear war within a framework of reason and faith, themselves experienced some very human emotions during this process. Bishop Hubbard, whom we heard from in the last chapter, mediated a discussion among bishops and presented amendments to the document at the Chicago conference. Asked if there was much uncertainty and ambivalence among the bishops, Hubbard readily responded, "Oh, I think there was! I think there was a great deal of angst on the part of the body, and on the part of individual bishops. In some sense, it seemed as if the whole issue was even beyond our ability to cope; you just feel a certain helplessness about it."

The bishops had available the latest political and strategic information, as well as resources from their religious tradition. Yet as Hubbard explains, "When you try to understand all the complexities involved, it tends to get overwhelming. You listen to defense experts, you listen to theologians, you listen to civil defense officials and peace activists. You get overwhelmed by the complexity of the issues, the divergence of viewpoints. Very often, arguments on the opposite side can seem very convincing. And you just kind of say, 'Well, who are *we* to make a pronouncement on something that seems so far beyond us?' "

However, Hubbard said that as individual bishops studied the issue, met for discussions, and circulated drafts of the document, a certain degree of confidence emerged. "As we got into it, we felt that there were certain guiding principles that are common to humanity, and a certain body of wisdom that the church has in her teachings and traditions, that *did* have something to say about this issue. And the more we studied it, the more confident we became that, while we didn't have all the answers, at least we had a direction to offer."

Deep religious conviction is the core of hope for many who work toward peace. Jim and Shelley Douglass (see Chapter 4) have committed their lives to "exploring nonviolence as a way of life." What keeps them going? Shelley is encouraged by the sense of gradual change in others' attitudes toward the nuclear issue, but quickly adds, "There's a big faith dimension. Even if we didn't see any results, faith in the Gospel and wanting to live that way give us inspiration."

But faith and hope do not lessen the urgency they feel for their task. "The main frustration I have," Jim admits, "is not having enough time to do all the work we're called to do. I don't feel any sense of despair or doubt. I feel we can deepen ourselves in this work to accomplish the kinds of things that are necessary."

Peacemakers

In facing the possibility of atomic catastrophe, both adults and young people need role models—leaders who can show them constructive ways of facing the challenge and can translate this courage into practical activities. Modern society finds itself in something of a predicament. Many of our youths' role models are sports and entertainment figures, most of whom do not fit the mold of opinion leaders from past generations. Video games, television, music, and movies have cut heavily into reading and family conversations as ways of learning about life. It's easy to become discouraged when there seems to be so few heroic figures to emulate. In the realm of religion, children and adults alike turn away. The saints of centuries ago seem too much a part of the past to inspire much hope when a problem as enormous as nuclear war surfaces.

If one of our tasks is to learn to experience despair, we must learn to do so from those who have conquered it. If the mass media are a gauge to the emotional pulse of the nation, certainly uneasiness and cynicism about world affairs abound.

Some fascinating observations were made by psychologist Kay Tooley on "The remembrance of things past: ingredients useful in the treatment of disorders resulting from unhappiness, rootlessness, and the fear of things to come."[8]

Tooley, who works primarily with suicidal patients, wondered why some people crumble under the pressure of human suffering while others do not. All of us have encountered the buoyancy, hopefulness, and strength with which some people in crisis-ridden lives cope, and even contribute to others.

Tooley studied the early life experiences of one very sorrowful, extreme group of young people: suicidal adolescents who had been adopted. What void in their lives made them unable to handle life's pressures?

Normal children build their identities from feedback they receive from loving parents, doting relatives, and other people in their lives. This is particularly true for the ages birth through four, because children usually can't remember details from that period and want to be told. Parents fill in this gap when children are older. Most will testify that children are endlessly fascinated and delighted by stories about their unrecollected childhood antics—"Tell me again how I gave all the bacon to the dog when I was little."[9]

Children need to lay claim to a personal history. They need to hear from adults what they were like and how they behaved in that vague and foggy past. This gives them hope to face the future: "The sense of a self unremembered but accepted as truly existing in the past inoculates against despair by suggesting that a new and unknown but lovable self could exist in the future."[10]

Children remind themselves of this reconstructed treasury of memories by keeping souvenirs of their youth, family snapshots, old toys, almost anything that symbolizes the past from which they have grown. The lack of this "historical identity" is visible in the treatment of suicidal teens whose parents, for whatever reasons, could not or would not recall details and anecdotes from the adolescent's pre-verbal past.

An analogy can be drawn, as our society finds itself in a position somewhat similar to that of suicidal, adopted adolescents. We face a future of doom and expected destruction. If the only way people can face life is by relying on a storehouse of memories of times when we were loved, where in our collective past can we find that inner treasury of meaning and affirmation?

Nuclear Anxiety and Feelings of Community

Most major religions place emphasis on community, the linking in friendship and fellowship with other believers. This tenet extends to both past and future generations, so that the religious person finds a certain unity with all of humanity. Most religious practices reinforce a sense of "the family of man" and feelings of solidarity with one another. In Christianity, for example, partakers of communion are spiritually joined with their God, and with fellow worshipers.

From a psychological perspective, does this participation in a strong, close-knit religious community help us cope with nuclear anxiety? A study conducted during the 1969 Israeli War produced surprising results.[11]

A psychologist compared two groups of kibbutzim children. One group lived in kibbutzim that were constantly under attack; thus, they lived daily with the possibility of death. The second group lived in safe areas, far from the fighting. The psychologist wanted to see if the children who lived under a state of siege were more anxious than those who lived in safety. It was a reasonable assumption, but it was not what he found: The shelled children were *no more anxious* than the safe children!

One reason thought to contribute to this occurrence is the structure of the kibbutz. This communal "gathering" provides membership, affiliation, togetherness, and security for a group of people who care for one another and who share similar fears and aspirations.

Hiding Behind Faith

Adults cannot be cautioned enough about the hazards of appearing too pious when discussing nuclear war with children (or with other adults). Glib responses like, "Don't worry, God will protect us," or "If Allah wills it" are inadequate. Regardless of the speaker's sincerity, children expect, and require, more substantive explanations. While the expression of an adult's faith in God is important, it should not be used as an excuse for not talking seriously about the subject.

Clinical social worker Donna DeMuth (see Chapter 4) sees two principal ways that religious feelings are handled in her workshops. Initially, some people are frightened when others begin to share their deep emotional responses to the thought of nuclear war. These people "put up a defensive posture with their peers, just like they do with kids. And part of that is religious: 'Oh, well, I know that God will take care of us.' It comes through in the workshops in a very shallow way, and it aggravates people. Other people get very, very angry when someone tries to reassure them that way."

Toward the end of the workshops, after participants have worked through many of their feelings, religious faith is expressed in an entirely different manner. "It's really fascinating how differently religious feelings can be used," DeMuth says. "In the first part of the workshops, the religious feelings expressed are really an avoidance. But after people have gone through the experience of feeling, and role-playing, and watching a film about nuclear war— after they've become a group, feel connected with one another, shared their guts together—*then* people will come in with more genuine feelings of hope. And that's where the religious beliefs of some people are very helpful."

Theologian James Fowler says faith is not a dogma, but a process that must develop if we are to mature. "I fear the possibility of a nuclear holocaust," he readily admits. "Who in his or her right mind doesn't? Especially after reading a book like Jonathan Schell's *The Fate of the Earth,* I am very sober about the precipitous edge to which we have come. And yet, my own master story keeps me from panic, despair, or paralysis. The conviction of the sovereignty of God is not just rhetoric for me. I believe that Being, to which we refer with the word God, is a power intending the fulfillment, not the destruction, of this experiment we call Earth. We are not alone. We are created for interdependence and partnership—with each other and with God. We dare not give in either to the despair or the arrogance of believing that our global future depends entirely on us. We are called to a level of responsibility that demands all that we have and are. But our responsibility is finally limited. That conviction helps me face the present and future with a measure of confidence and genuine joy."[12]

Active Mastery

How can adults who work with children bring this down to a practical level? Dan O'Donnell, a special education teacher and a religion instructor for more than ten years, commented on this: "A normal part of growing up is for kids to learn they *can* affect other people's lives. They can affect it in good ways, or in bad ways." O'Donnell reflected on his work as a teacher with violent inner-city youngsters. "Most of the feedback these kids got was how they were a nuisance or a burden to an already overburdened adult. They grew up without the experience of pleasing others. As a result, many of them developed an 'I don't give a damn, I'll do what I want' attitude. So in the classroom, you try to get them to feel that all the little things they could do—clipping out an article, telling a story, helping wash down the chalkboard—were actions that contributed to the group. That made a difference."

O'Donnell sees one of the objectives of religious education as helping young people see how they fit into the community at large, "to create experiences where they can see how their little bit makes a difference, what happens when their contribution *is* given to the community, or withheld from the community."

Once this occurs, he says, "it's not such a big logical jump when the whole nuclear thing comes up. Kids can be a little more hopeful about changing something so vast and global once they've learned of the significant and positive impact they can have in a smaller setting."

Optimism versus Hope

Optimism and hope are not synonyms, although the words are often used interchangeably. It's especially easy to confuse optimism with hope when the nuclear threat is considered.

Optimism is a feeling, a tendency to expect the best possible outcome. Its opposite is pessimism, which can range from a sense of uneasiness to forebodings of gloom and doom. *Hope,* on the other hand, is more than a feeling. Hope is a commitment, a ground for expectation. It is confidence in, and dedication to, the future. Hope looks at all the things in the present that can be done to bring about a better future. Hope means not giving up even when you feel like it. The opposite of hope is not pessimism, it is despair. Despair is the utter lack of hope, the belief that all effort will be to no avail.[13]

Although we can't support our assumption with formal data (and it would make a most interesting area for research), we would guess that many people working to bring about a solution to the nuclear weapons issue feel a sense of pessimism, yet are inspired to work on in hope.

In *Man Against Himself,* psychiatrist Karl Menninger tells of an experiment performed with rats placed into a tank of water. Rats that were given no visible means of escape sometimes swam for hours before drowning. Those that were permitted to see the possibility of escape—a little ramp at the top of the tank, just beyond their reach—often swam several hours longer.

On a human level, hope flushes us with strength, energy, and emotional resources to square our shoulders against hard times and forge through them. This story by Robert Mills, an administrator at Temple Sholom in Chicago, conveys the enigmatic power of hope.

"A plainly dressed man came into the Temple seeking 'help,' which usually is synonymous with money. He was in the building because his wife was terminally ill at St. Joseph Hospital. He said that he prayed daily in the hospital chapel, but that day he felt he wanted to be in a Jewish setting.

"I took him to our chapel and gave him a prayer book and sat with him for awhile, establishing a human contact that assured him that others could feel the pain, and then left him with his prayer book, alone in the chapel. Some twenty minutes later he emerged with an appearance of reassurance on his face. He left the building confidently after telling me that this had done him much good and that he was sure it would help his wife.

"Somehow I believed him. Yes, this was good for his wife, but why? On one level, we might say that his prayer was an expression of hope, in which under some miraculous circumstances there would be a direct response resulting in the fulfillment of his wishes.

This would be magical thinking, and, although such thinking would be a helpful emotional experience, there would be little to satisfy one intellectually. Perhaps this man's experience of hope affected him in such a way that his becoming strengthened was now to become a part of his very bearing. Conceivably, this reawakened strength could be transmitted to his wife, and in that mysterious way in which one human adds strength, courage, moral fiber to a significant other human, activate the response that helps to encourage physical recovery and/or emotional stamina. Some of his own reaffirmed hope might in this manner become hope for her also."[14]

This man's hope helped him to face what he needed to face.

Edward Stein, professor of pastoral psychology at the San Francisco Theological Seminary at San Anselmo, gives another example of hope. "When I was on sabbatical at the University of Hawaii, a young engineer about thirty years of age came to the door. He was handsome but depressed-looking. He had been directed to me by another professor. He said, 'What do you have to say to someone who is about to die?' He had a terminal illness and was having to give up his work, his girl, and his life. One evening he called me to his apartment. He couldn't see the use of going on. I was groping for some answer. Casually, I asked, 'Why don't you adopt a war orphan overseas?' He nearly fell off his chair leaping at the idea. He had a goal, whether he lived or died. There was a meaningful continuity, *some* future. The change in him was visible. He could perpetuate life in some way."[15]

These examples illustrate the psychological value of hope. Its importance was emphasized by E. J. Dionne, a political reporter for the *New York Times:* "Hope, it seemed to me, always got shortchanged in the great trinity of Christian virtues, even though it is central to the orientation that a Christian brings to every action in his or her life."[16]

Beyond all else that has been said in this chapter, another dimension needs to be acknowledged. One implicit message of this book, and indeed almost any book on this subject, is that every person, adult or child, can take certain steps that cumulatively will either increase or decrease the chances of nuclear war. Psychologically speaking, these steps (and they are many and varied) give those who make them a feeling of being "in control" of events that appear to be headed greatly out of control.

It's a form of faith: reason, good sense, and working together will bring things about. However rational this approach seems, we are advised that the scope of what is possible regarding a nuclear disaster may already be beyond man's ability to change.

"I don't think that this problem is going to be solved by a lot of maneuvering, conferences, and summit meetings," Father Theodore Hesburgh contends. He has devoted more than three decades of his life to working at national and international levels to promote peace and social justice.

Nuclear war, Hesburgh believes, "is ultimately so important, and represents so great an evil, that it's going to have to be faced by prayer and fasting." Children, he says, "can actually do something—they can pray for something. We all have to commit ourselves to this like the bishops have. And kids can understand that."

·6·

Keeping Things in Perspective

In this book, we have said that nuclear war is on the minds of many young people today. The research supports this finding with hard-to-deny evidence. What's more, anyone who watches television, goes to the movies, reads popular periodicals or listens to contemporary rock music knows that mention of nuclear warfare is frequently made.

So why bother with it? Why dwell on such an unhappy subject? Many grown-ups believe that the best approach to take with children is to ignore the issue entirely, or at least remain ambivalent to it. This reaction has merit, at least to the extent that "talking to kids about nuclear war" should not take place too early, and should not become an adult obsession. Many children, though, in response to the stimuli of their environment, *do* have questions; in some cases, they're also afraid. Childlike curiosity or a genuine dread of atomic destruction, the fact that children think about nuclear war is one of the few certainties in an uncertain nuclear age.

We believe it is crucial for young people to receive correct information and needed emotional support from the adults who love them and/or are important in their lives. These people— parents, relatives, schoolteachers, church officers, favorite neighbors, whomever—can place the potential for nuclear annihilation in its proper context: that is, a fact of all our lives.

Dr. Benjamin Spock, child-care author and activist, is convinced that fear of nuclear war is a pediatric issue. Looking back on the 60s, when children were first subjected to the threat of nuclear war in the form of air-raid drills, and students taught to hide under their desks for protection, Spock says, "This is a terrible thing to do to children, to kid 'em along into thinking that crawling under a desk will save them."

Rather than teach kids how to hide from bombs, Spock suggests a better way to alleviate children's anxiety over the nuclear threat is to let them see their parents doing something. "Join an anti-nuke group. Join a pro-nuke group. Do anything but cower under the desk."

"I think it's good for children to know their parents have beliefs and are not powerless, waiting for annihilation. The healthy biological response to danger is to do something."[1]

Do What's Relevant for You

Too frequently, in our attempt to convey the urgency of the situation and motivate others to work against nuclear weapons, we become intolerant and rigid. Psychiatrist Harris Peck describes how his involvement with the peace movement grew, and how he helps others embark on a course of action that makes sense to them.

"I am what's called a late bloomer. Not long ago, I was one of the 'silent ones.' If you had asked me a couple of years ago what I was doing about my concern—which was considerable—I would have had to say, 'Essentially, nothing.'

"My wife was getting really very angry at me. I'd say, 'Gee, I've gotta do something.' I was getting increasingly tense, irritable. I wasn't feeling good, I really wasn't. And I would have immediately made a brilliant diagnostic appraisal if it had been somebody else. But I continued stewing for several months."[2]

Dr. Peck eventually decided to do what he was comfortable with professionally: running small group sessions. "I believe small groups and large groups have relevance," he reports. "The nice part about a large meeting is that you just have to get yourself there, and feel a little bit virtuous. You can be anonymous. And when you see a lot of people who share your concern, you think, 'Maybe *they'll* do something.' " But Peck prefers small groups. "Because once people acknowledge how scared they are—*and the emotions of fear and anger and sadness are signals to us that there's something we need to do*—once they admit how they are keeping themselves from acting on those feelings, from using those emotions for problem-solving, then they begin to do something."[3]

What he doesn't like to hear from people are statements like: "I'm in the freeze movement. How come you're not signing this petition?" or "We're marching next weekend. Why aren't you?" He believes it is wrong to push people into activities that may not be meaningful or appropriate for them.

"You have to look at *you*, who *you* are," he emphasizes. "You think the most important thing is to talk with your kids so they don't . . . ," "You want to see if your minister will . . . ," "You want to read . . . ," "You want to educate . . . ," and so on. He stresses that people must start where they are.

Dr. Peck encourages people to use their individual creative talents or professional expertise to break their cycle of passivity or silence. "Start to act, but don't do it by yourself," he cautions. "For most of us, it's too scary. Find somebody, *somebody,* that you can tell it to and say: 'Would you come back in a week and see if I've done it, and encourage me if I haven't?' We need each other badly, to live, not die."[4]

When children see adults confronting nuclear issues in mature and responsible ways, then the situation does not seem so awesome, overwhelming, and out-of-control. They begin to have hope in the future. Whether the adults they love and trust most are active in the peace movement or speak out strongly in support of our nation's nuclear policies is not all that important to young people; what *is* important is that these adults are taking whatever steps that are meaningful to them to help prevent a nuclear war. Regardless of their political or moral beliefs, these adults have faced the problem. And kids do notice.

An adult with many years of professional experience in counseling disturbed children made this comparison between their problems and the fear nuclear war summons in all of us:

> The children I work with are in therapy because of circumstances outside of their control. There is enormous family pathology and emotional upheaval in their lives. It's just too much for these little kids to deal with, much less change. They don't understand what is happening. In the face of such odds, they give up. Quit. Their despair takes any of a number of antisocial behaviors and causes all kinds of grief and misery.
>
> What we try and do with these kids is to help them see all the little things they can do which are important and can give their life some meaning and direction. When they begin to learn that cleaning their room, helping plan a field trip, playing with their friends are all activities that can make them feel better about themselves . . . then that's progress! They begin to regain control over their lives.
>
> Nuclear war is surprisingly similar. It's also so overwhelming that we want to forget about it, give up and hope it goes away. It won't, and this 'What's the use?' attitude won't help a thing. I think that by showing kids that the little things we do can make a difference and can help get things back under control is a tremendous example and inspiration. It gives the kids hope.

A big step for many adults, especially parents, is weighing all the pros and cons of discussing nuclear weapons and nuclear war with their children. This is an important process, and a valuable one. If, after such reflection and deliberation, parents opt *not* to talk about nuclear issues with their children, they should remember that that's one of the choices. If they are simply too uncomfortable discussing the subject, then there need be no added pressure to do so, nor any guilt for not doing so. (It is one area, however, where parents are well-advised to confer with their spouse before talking with their youngsters.)

For adults who decide to take the next step—responding to children's questions as they arise or broaching the subject themselves when they feel it is timely—we have presented several practical approaches we think will be helpful. Much of this advice is obvious, common-sense information for adults who care about children: listen to their questions, determine what's on their minds, and talk with them about it. All children need to have their love affirmed, and the methods we have recommended demonstrate parental love and caring. Children ages six through twelve may raise questions prompted by environmental cues, questions which can be answered in several ways. Older teens, in particular, need the opportunity to make their own decisions and arrive at their own conclusions.

For readers with religious convictions, we've tried to explain some of the human emotions and moral dilemmas which surface when nuclear war and weapons are discussed. We hope that these people will be better able to understand these two dimensions once they've considered this material. When adults are prepared to discuss nuclear issues on a factual basis as well as an emotional one, then they'll be more confident and more effective when they speak to children about these matters.

Beyond describing some of the general political/ethical postures most frequently taken, we did not go into intimate detail about the wealth of factual information available on nuclear issues. In fact, we suspect that the sheer volume of this material oftentimes discourages further investigation. We did consider including a short appendix of suggested reading, but the task of balancing this offering to appeal to so many different opinions was not practical. Instead, we encourage readers to seek out additional information on their own. This has the advantage of putting readers in touch with other living, breathing beings who are knowledgeable on the subject.

Having said that, we will recommend one book which we consider an excellent primer. *Living with Nuclear Weapons*, written by a team of Harvard scholars, is uncomplicated and easy to understand. This 268-page text approaches the problem from a historical perspective, explains some of the major military strategies surrounding nuclear weapons, and presents nonpartisan analyses of all sides of the nuclear debate. With an introduction by Harvard president Derek Bok, this book is especially appropriate for teenagers who want to understand the problems of the nuclear age.

We hope that our book, *Talking to Children About Nuclear War,* will not gather dust on your bookshelf. It's meant to be reread, dogeared, passed along to other adults, criticized, and heeded. The advice we offer is not sacred; it's not carved in stone atop some mountain. Rather, it's meant merely as a guide for your consideration. We hope it inspires thoughtful reflection. We sincerely believe that the more you think about nuclear war, the more you'll want to involve your children in thinking about ways to prevent it.

In conclusion, the authors go on record as saying that thinking and talking about nuclear war is but one part of growing up. Kids still need to be kids. That means birthday parties and circuses, bicycles and roller skates, baseball games and kites, hot baths and Sunday comics, family picnics and school plays, first dates and junior proms, piggyback rides and firm curfews, driver's ed and newspaper routes, butterfly collections and skinned knees, secret hideouts and best friends. While children's concerns about nuclear war must also be met, adults will be truly supportive when they are honest, life-affirming, and, most of all, hopeful.

Notes

Chapter 1 / Wanting to "Do Something"

1. M. Howard, "Nuclear Bookshelf," *Harpers,* February 1983, pp. 65–70.
2. Frances Peavey and Charles Varon, "How to Talk with Your Children about Nuclear War," 1982 (Article published by Interhelp, a nonpartisan organization, P.O. Box 331, Northampton, MA 01060).
3. Ronald J. Sider and Richard K. Taylor, *Nuclear Holocaust and Christian Hope* (Downers Grove, Ill.: InterVarsity Press, 1982), p. 11.
4. Jeffrey Stinson and Eric Brazel, "Bishops Take Nuke Letter to Pulpits," *USA Today,* 23 May 1983, sec. 1.
5. "Peace Games," *Working Woman,* June 1983, p. 134.
6. Study conducted by Ronald Doctor, a psychologist at California State University at Northridge, reported by Norma Peterson, in "Nuclear War: A Modern-day Bogeyman," *USA Today,* 16 November 1983, Life Section.
7. Anne Frank, *Anne Frank: The Diary of a Young Girl* (New York: Simon and Schuster, Pocket Books, 1953), p. 70.
8. Tapio Nummenmaa, "Mental Representation of Events: War and Peace," in Marianne Kahnert, David Pitt, and Ilkka Taipale, eds., *Children and War: Proceedings of Symposium at Siuntio Baths, Finland 24.3-27.3, 1983* (published by the Geneve International Peace Research Institute, International Peace Bureau, and Peace Union of Finland), p. 167.
9. From personal correspondence with Mrs. Betty Bumpers (Peace Links Worldwide, 723½ Eighth Street, S.E., Washington, D.C. 20003), 15 August 1983.

10. Ibid.
11. From telephone conversation with the Rev. Theodore M. Hesburgh, University of Notre Dame, Notre Dame, Indiana, 29 August 1983.
12. From personal interview with Nessa Rabin (Children's Campaign for Nuclear Disarmament, Box 55, RD 1, Plainfield, VT 05667), 4 July 1983.
13. Strobe Talbott, "Playing for the Future," *Time,* 18 March 1983, p. 17.
14. Frank, *Diary of a Young Girl,* p. 11.
15. Judy Langford Carter, "You Can Try to Make the World Safer for Your Children," *Redbook,* July 1982, pp. 28–32.
16. Eric Chivian, "The Bomb Threat and Child Development" (Report delivered at the Sixtieth Annual Meeting of the American Orthopsychiatric Association, Boston, 4–8 April 1983).

Chapter 2 / It's a Fact: Kids Think About Nuclear War

1. Michael J. Carey, "Psychological Fallout," *The Bulletin of the Atomic Scientists,* January 1982, pp. 20–24.
2. Tony Wagner, "Why Nuclear Education?" *Educational Leadership,* May 1983, p. 40.
3. Chivian, "The Bomb Threat" [n. 16 in chap. 1 above].
4. *USA Today,* 20 July 1983, Life section.
5. Natalie Gittelson, "The Fear That Haunts Our Children," *McCalls,* May 1982, p. 77.
6. Ibid.
7. Sibylle Escalona, "Issues and Solutions: The Nuclear Threat" (Remarks made as moderator of the April 7 evening session, the Sixtieth Annual Meeting of the American Orthopsychiatric Association, Boston, 4–8 April 1983).
8. William Beardslee and John Mack, "The Impact on Children and Adolescents of Nuclear Developments," American Psychiatric Association Task Force Report #20, *The Psychosocial Aspects of Nuclear Developments,* 1981. (Complete report is available from the American Psychiatric Association, 1700 Eighteenth Street, N.W., Washington, D.C. For information, write to the Publication Sales Division.)
9. John Mack, "The Perception of U.S.-Soviet Intentions and Other Psychological Dimensions of the Nuclear Arms Race," *American Journal of Orthopsychiatry* 52/4 (October 1982): 592.
10. From personal correspondence with Penny Jaworski, coordinator

of Youth Activities for the Archdiocese of Chicago, 19 July 1983.
11. Chivian, "The Bomb Threat."
12. Ibid.
13. Milton Schwebel, "Effects of the Nuclear War Threat on Children and Teenagers: Implications for Professionals," *American Journal of Orthopsychiatry* 52/4 (October 1982): 609.
14. Chivian, "The Bomb Threat."
15. Vivienne Verdon-Roe, "Nuclear Threat: Our Children Are Afraid," *Presbyterian Survey,* January 1983, p. 10. (The 25-minute documentary film, "In the Nuclear Shadow: What Can the Children Tell Us?" can be bought or rented in 16mm film and video cassette versions from The Educational Film and Video Project, a nonprofit distributing company at 1725 B Seabright Ave., Santa Cruz, CA 90562.)
16. Ibid., 11.
17. Ibid.
18. Ibid.
19. Ibid., 12.
20. Ibid.
21. Ibid.
22. Mack, "The Perception of U.S.-Soviet Intentions," p. 597.
23. Artur Petrovski, "Soviet Children and War," in Marianne Kahnert et al., eds., *Children and War* [n. 8 in chap. 1 above], p. 85.

Chapter 3 / Family Vulnerability

1. Benina F. Gould, "Families and the Nuclear Threat," 1983 (Paper issued by the Family Therapy Institute of California, 3738 Mt. Diablo Blvd., Suite 100, Layfayette, CA 94549).
2. Philip G. Zimbardo, "The Age of Indifference," *Psychology Today,* August 1980, p. 72.
3. Steven Zeitlin, "Families and the Threat of Nuclear War: Facing Our Vulnerability Together" (Presentation at the Sixtieth Annual Meeting of the American Orthopsychiatric Association, Boston, 4–8 April 1983).
4. Ibid.
5. Verdon-Roe, "Nuclear Threat" [n. 15 in chap. 2 above], p. 10.
6. Pastor Ken Sutherland, 15 May 1983, correspondence and transcript of youth group discussion on nuclear issues, Grace Lutheran Church, Salem, Oregon.

7. Albert Furtwangler, "Growing Up Nuclear," *The Bulletin of the Atomic Scientists,* January 1981, p. 44.
8. Ibid., 45.
9. Ibid., 48.
10. Robert Jay Lifton and Richard Falk, *Indefensible Weapons: The Political and Psychological Case Against Nuclearism* (New York: Basic Books, 1982), p. 68.
11. Mack, "The Perception of U.S.-Soviet Intentions" [n. 9 in chap. 2 above], p. 598.
12. Verdon-Roe, "Nuclear Threat," p. 12.
13. Lifton and Falk, *Indefensible Weapons,* p. 71.
14. Verdon-Roe, "Nuclear Threat," p. 13.
15. Ibid.
16. George Fitchett, "Wisdom and Folly in Death and Dying," *Journal of Religion and Health* 19/3 (Fall 1980): 203–13.

Chapter 4 / Talking Together

1. From telephone conversation with Mrs. Betty Bumpers, Little Rock, Ark., 11 August 1983.
2. Peavey and Varon, "How to Talk with Your Children" [n. 2 in chap. 1 above].
3. Ibid.
4. E. H. Waechter, "Children's Awareness of Fatal Illness," *American Journal of Nursing* 71 (1971): 1168–72.
5. "Let's Talk About Death," *Christopher News Notes,* no. 206.
6. Elisabeth Kübler-Ross, *Living with Death and Dying* (New York: Macmillan, 1982), p. 4.
7. Thomas Powers, "What to Tell the Kids," *Commonweal,* 6 November 1981, p. 616.
8. Ibid.
9. Ibid., 617.
10. Schwebel, "Effects of the Nuclear War Threat" [n. 13 in chap. 2 above], pp. 615–16.
11. Ann Japenga, "Alleviating Children's Fears of Nuclear War," *Los Angeles Times,* 30 November 1982, sec. 5.
12. Kübler-Ross, *Living with Death,* p. 16.
13. John Darr, "The Impact of the Nuclear Threat on Children," *American Journal of Orthopsychiatry* 33 (1963): 203–4.
14. William Van Ornum and John B. Mordock, *Crisis Counseling with*

Children and Adolescents: A Guide for Nonprofessional Counselors (New York: Continuum, 1983).

15. Selma Fraiberg, *The Magic Years: Understanding and Handling the Problems of Early Childhood* (New York: Scribner's, 1959).

16. Elizabeth Geleerd, "The Psychiatric Care of Children in Wartime," *American Journal of Orthopsychiatry* 12 (1942): 587–93.

17. Ibid.

18. Virginia E. Pomeranz with Dodi Schulz, "Answering Your Child's Questions About Sex," *Parents,* August 1983, p. 87.

19. Ibid.

20. "What Shall We Tell the Children?" 1983 (Booklet produced by Parenting in a Nuclear Age, 6501 Telegraph Avenue, Oakland, CA 94609), p. 10.

21. Metta Winter, "Talking to Kids," *Ms.* Magazine, August 1983, p. 85.

22. "Teaching About Nuclear War," *Newsweek,* 18 July 1983, p. 78.

23. Roberta Snow, "Issues and Solutions: The Nuclear Threat" (Report delivered at the Sixtieth Annual Meeting of the American Orthopsychiatric Association, Boston, 4–8 April 1983).

24. Schwebel, "Effects of the Nuclear War Threat," p. 616.

25. Snow, "Issues and Solutions."

26. Ibid.

27. Phyllis Schlafly, "Kids Made to Knock Nukes," *The Daily Freeman* (Kingston, New York), 25 July 1983, Editorial section.

28. Gordon Oliver, "Teaching Peace to Our Children," *National Catholic Reporter,* 24 December 1982, p. 13.

Chapter 5 / From Despair to Hope

1. Joanna Rogers Macy, "How to Deal with Despair," *New Age,* 1979, pp. 40–45.

2. Ibid., 40.

3. Ibid., 42.

4. Ibid., 41.

5. Ibid., 42.

6. Ibid., 44.

7. Morris West, *The Clowns of God* (New York: Bantam Books, 1982), pp. 294–95.

8. Kay Tooley, "The Remembrance of Things Past: On the Collection and Recollection of Ingredients Useful in the Treatment of Disorders Resulting from Unhappiness, Rootlessness, and the Fear of

Things to Come," *American Journal of Orthopsychiatry* 48 (1978): 174–82.

9. Ibid.

10. Ibid.

11. Avner Ziv and Ruth Israeli, "Effects of Bombardment on the Manifest Anxiety Level of Children Living in Kibbutzim," *Journal of Consulting and Clinical Psychology* 40 (1973): 287–91.

12. Linda Lawrence, "James Fowler: Stages of Faith," *Psychology Today*, November 1983, pp. 56–62.

13. M. Brewster Smith, "Hope and Despair: Keys to the Socio-Psychodynamics of Youth," *American Journal of Orthopsychiatry* 53/3 (July 1983): 388–98.

14. Robert Mills, "An Anatomy of Hope," *Journal of Religion and Health* 18/1 (1979): 49–52.

15. Edward V. Stein, "Faith, Hope, and Suicide," *Journal of Religion and Health* 10/3 (1971): 214–25.

16. E. J. Dionne, Jr., "Hope and Fantasy: The Missing Virtue," *Commonweal*, 13 February 1981, pp. 68–69.

Chapter 6 / Keeping Things in Perspective

1. Japenga, "Alleviating Children's Fears" [n. 10 in chap. 4 above].

2. Harris B. Peck, "A Small Group Strategy for Dealing with Denial of the Nuclear Threat" (Presentation at the Sixtieth Annual Meeting of the American Orthopsychiatric Association, Boston, 4–8 April 1983).

3. Ibid.

4. Ibid.

Of Related Interest from Crossroad/Continuum

William Van Ornum and John B. Mordock
Crisis Counseling with Children and Adolescents
A Guide for Non-Professional Counselors
Introduction by Eugene Kennedy

Philip J. Murnion, Editor
Catholics and Nuclear War
The U.S. Catholic Bishops'
Pastoral Letter on War and Peace
Foreword by Theodore M. Hesburgh

James W. Douglass
Lightning East to West
Jesus, Gandhi, and the Nuclear Age
Foreword by Archbishop Raymond Hunthausen